NELSON MANDELA

THE AUTHORISED COMIC BOOK

NELSON MANDELA FOUNDATION

WITH

UMLANDO WEZITHOMBE

JONATHAN BALL PUBLISHERS
JOHANNESBURG & CAPE TOWN

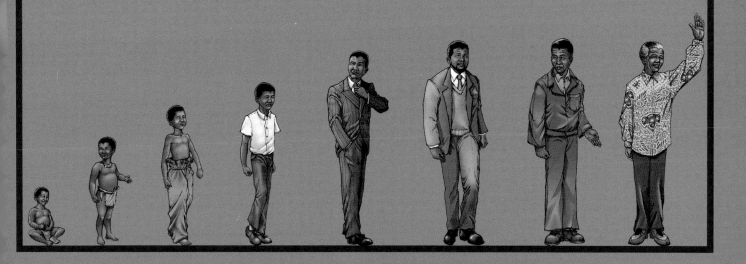

CONTENTS

1
A SON OF THE EASTERN CAPE

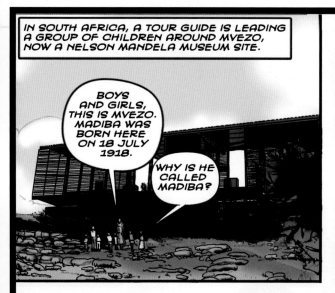

IN SOUTH AFRICA, A TOUR GUIDE IS LEADING A GROUP OF CHILDREN AROUND MVEZO, NOW A NELSON MANDELA MUSEUM SITE.

BOYS AND GIRLS, THIS IS MVEZO. MADIBA WAS BORN HERE ON 18 JULY 1918.

WHY IS HE CALLED MADIBA?

MADIBA IS NELSON ROLIHLAHLA MANDELA'S CLAN NAME.

NELSON'S FATHER, MPHAKANYISWA, GADLA MANDELA WAS THE CHIEF OF MVEZO.

HERE ARE THE REMAINS OF THE HOUSE WHERE HE WAS BORN.

HIS MOTHER, NOSEKENI, WAS HIS FATHER'S THIRD WIFE.

THE YOUNG ROLIHLAHLA'S FATHER WAS IN BIG TROUBLE...

BRING ME MPHAKANYISWA NOW!!

YES SIR !

CHIEF MPHAKANYISWA HAD NOT REPORTED A TRIBAL MATTER TO THE MAGISTRATE.

THEY ALSO PLAYED OTHER GAMES.

COME ON BUTHI, ALL THE WAY!!!

SLIDING DOWN ROCKS WAS A BIG FAVOURITE!

WHOOOO!!

...AND HUNTING.

YES YOU GOT IT!

...ALSO FISHING.

THE MOTHER OF YOUR FOREFATHER WHO WAS NAMED MANDELA, LED THE THEMBU IN THE FIGHT AGAINST THE INVADING WHITES.

AT NIGHT, THE CHILDREN WOULD HUDDLE AROUND THE COOKING FIRE AND LISTEN TO STORIES.

THE CLANS GATHERED AT THE GREAT PLACE.

MY PEOPLE ARE WORRIED...

ALL THAT LISTENING HAS MADE YOU HUNGRY ROLIHLAHLA!

EVERY VOICE WAS HEARD, BUT WOMEN COULD ONLY BE OBSERVERS.

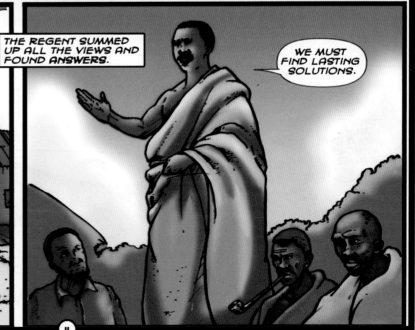

THE REGENT SUMMED UP ALL THE VIEWS AND FOUND ANSWERS.

WE MUST FIND LASTING SOLUTIONS.

11

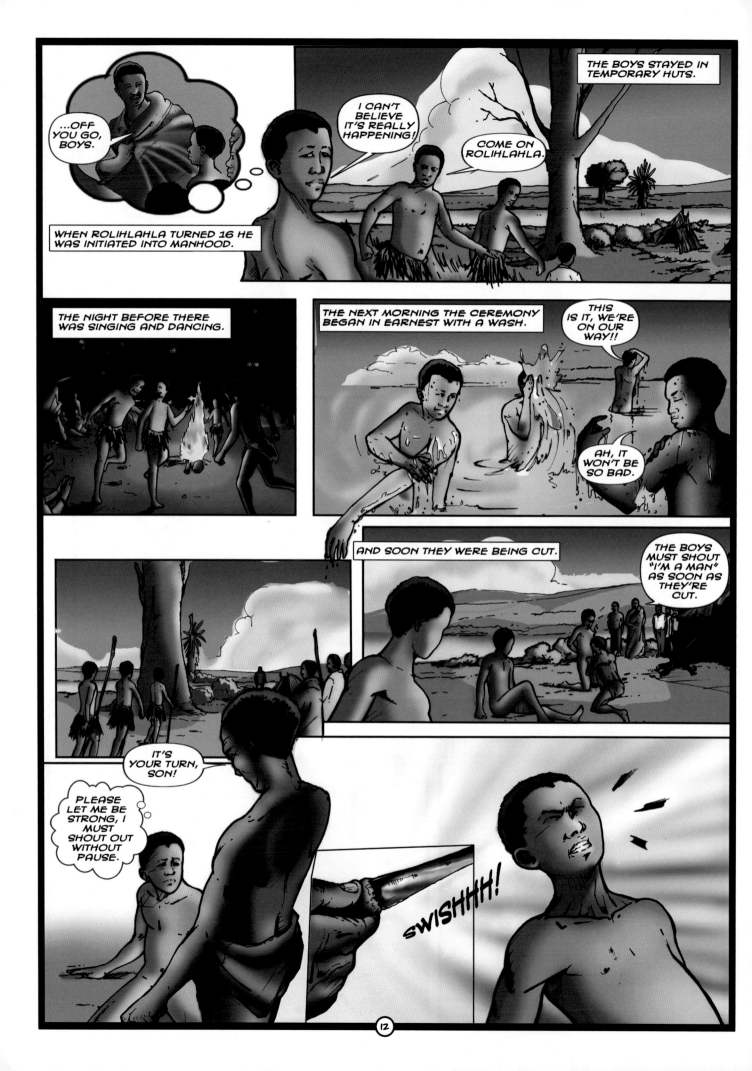

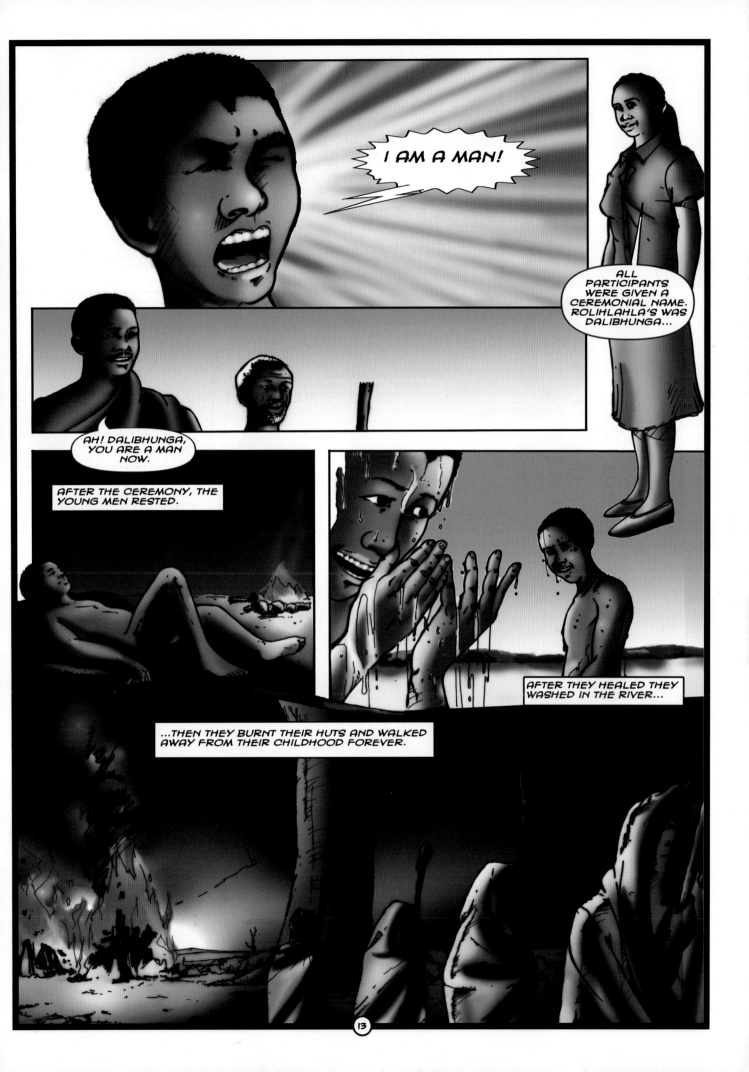

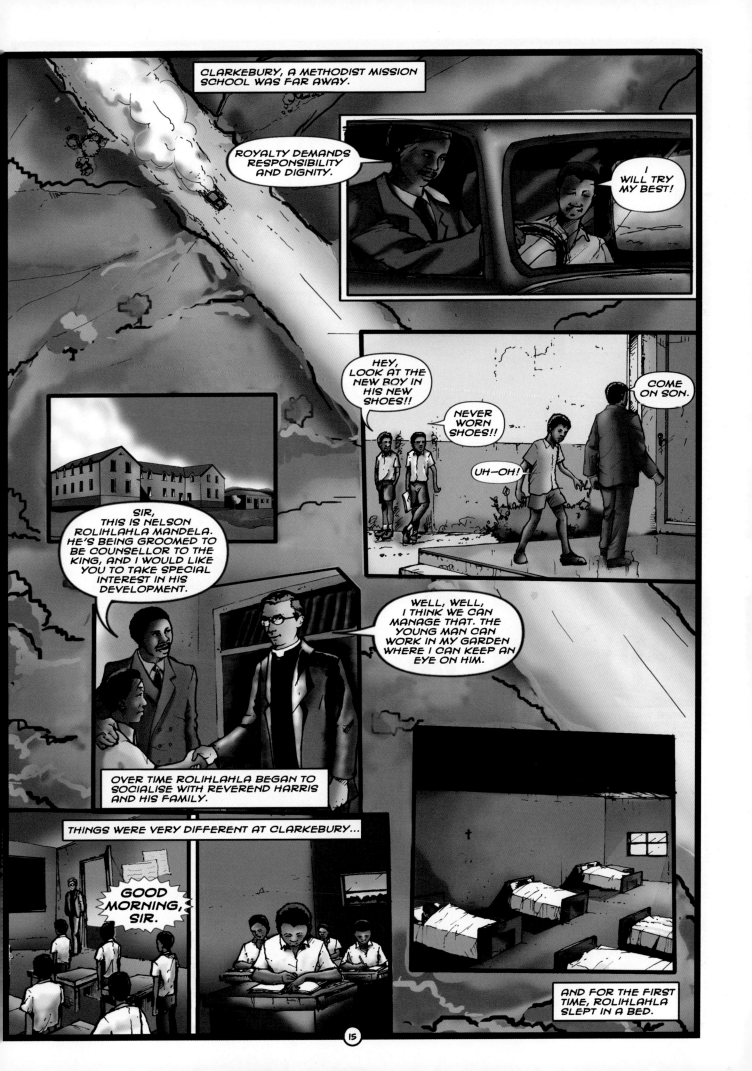

THE NEXT STEP WAS FORT HARE UNIVERSITY.

HE STUDIED ENGLISH, POLITICS, ANTHROPOLOGY, ROMAN DUTCH LAW AND NATIVE ADMINISTRATION.

I'VE BEEN MEANING TO INTRODUCE YOU TWO,

ROLIHLAHLA NELSON MANDELA, MEET KAISER MATANZIMA.

HE ALSO MET OLIVER TAMBO.

OLIVER, WITHOUT YOU WE WOULD HAVE LOST THAT DEBATE...

HE LOVED BALLROOM DANCING, AND SOMETIMES ROLIHLAHLA AND HIS FRIENDS SNEAKED OUT TO PARTIES...

MAY I HAVE THIS DANCE?

YOU DANCE BEAUTIFULLY...

ONCE HE DISCOVERED THAT HE WAS DANCING WITH A PROFESSOR'S WIFE.

HE ENJOYED SOCIALISING WITH FRIENDS.

HE PLAYED SOCCER, RAN CROSS COUNTRY, JOINED THE DRAMA SOCIETY AND GOT INVOLVED IN STUDENT POLITICS.

ROLIHLAHLA CONVEYED THE NEWS TO THE REGENT.

...SO HE SAID IF I DON'T TAKE UP MY SEAT IN THE COUNCIL I MUST LEAVE...

WHAT! I CAN'T BELIEVE WHAT I'M HEARING. YOU WILL GO BACK TO UNIVERSITY!

BIG CITY, YOU HAVE TO SEE IT...!

HE WAS RE-UNITED WITH JUSTICE IN THE HOLIDAYS.

HEY JUSTICE! WAIT!

SO HOW WAS CAPE TOWN?

SOON THEY WERE BACK TO THEIR OLD WAYS AGAIN...

...TRYING TO IMPRESS THE GIRLS...

...ATTENDING CHURCH.

ONE SUNDAY, THE REGENT HAD A SURPRISE FOR THEM.

THINGS WERE ABOUT TO CHANGE...

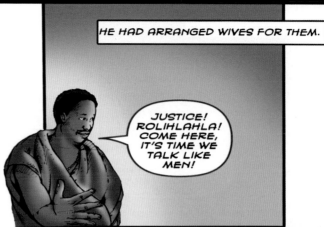

HE HAD ARRANGED WIVES FOR THEM.

JUSTICE! ROLIHLAHLA! COME HERE, IT'S TIME WE TALK LIKE MEN!

THIS IS HOW IT WILL BE... AND THAT'S FINAL.

THERE IS ONLY ONE THING TO DO... WE HAVE TO RUN AWAY.

TO JOHANNESBURG...

...WE'VE GOT NO TIME TO WASTE.

WHAT ABOUT MONEY?

DON'T WORRY, I HAVE AN IDEA!

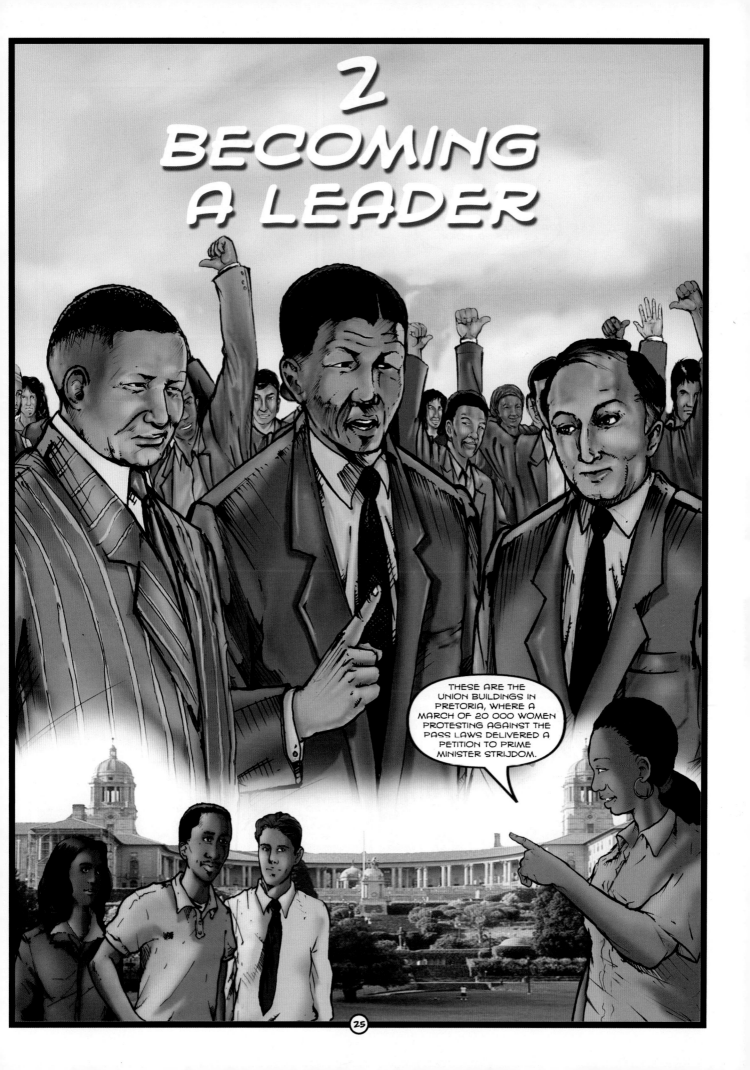

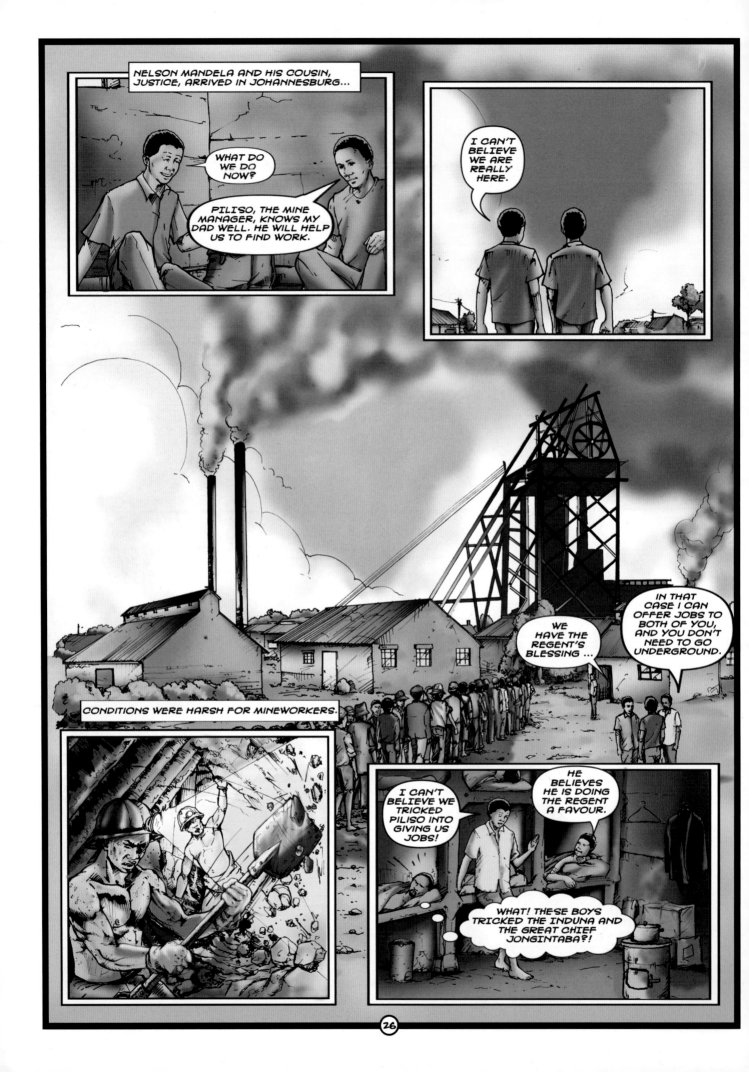

REGENT!

ROLIHLAHLA, I HEAR YOU HAVE FOUND A HOME FOR YOURSELF...

THE REGENT VISITED JOHANNESBURG IN 1941.

AFTER I STOLE THE CATTLE, I WAS WORRIED THAT THE BOND BETWEEN US WAS BROKEN.

NO, ROLIH... I WILL SUPP... BUT I NEED TO... HOME. I A... WELL...

IN THE WINTER OF 1942 THE REGENT DIED. JUSTICE AND MANDELA READ OF HIS DEATH IN THE NEWSPAPER. THE TELEGRAM SENT TO THEM DID NOT ARRIVE.

WE MUST HURRY, WE MAY HAVE ALREADY MISSED THE FUNERAL.

HE LOOKED UNWELL WHEN HE VISITED. I SHOULD HAVE GONE HOME THEN...

I SHOULD HAVE APPRECIATED THE REGENT WHILE HE WAS ALIVE. HE TREATED ME AS A SON.

SADLY, MANDELA AND JUSTICE ARRIVED AT THE GREAT PLACE A DAY AFTER THE REGENT'S FUNERAL...

AFTER A WEEK MANDELA SAID GOODBYE TO HIS MOTHER AND JUSTICE WHO WAS TO SUCCEED THE REGENT.

STAY WELL.

BACK IN JOHANNESBURG, RADEBE WAS SURPRISED THAT MANDELA RETURNED.

IT IS GOOD TO BE BACK!

I STILL HAVE MANY RIVERS TO CROSS...

29

IN 1943, MANDELA GRADUATED WITH A BA DEGREE AT FORT HARE. HIS MOTHER, NOSEKENI, HIS NEPHEW, KAISER MATANZIMA, AND THE REGENT'S WIDOW, NO-ENGLAND, WERE THERE TO WISH HIM WELL.

NELSON, YOU ARE NEEDED HERE NOW. WHY DON'T YOU STAY?

MANDELA DECLINED. HE RETURNED TO THE CITY TO CONTINUE HIS LAW STUDIES AT WITS UNIVERSITY. THIS WAS A DIFFICULT TIME FOR HIM, WITH MANY NEW FRIENDSHIPS, AND MANY HUMILIATIONS.

MANDELA ARRIVED LATE FOR CLASS ON OCCASION...

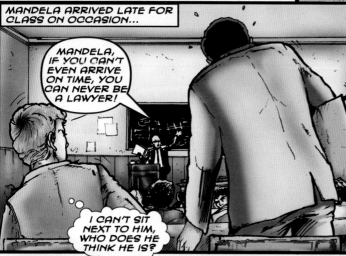

MANDELA, IF YOU CAN'T EVEN ARRIVE ON TIME, YOU CAN NEVER BE A LAWYER!

I CAN'T SIT NEXT TO HIM, WHO DOES HE THINK HE IS?

MANDELA WAS THE ONLY AFRICAN IN HIS CLASS. HE COULD NOT USE THE SPORTS FIELDS, SWIMMING POOL, CAFETERIA OR RESIDENCES. THESE WERE FOR WHITES ONLY!

MANDELA HAD A MIX OF EXPERIENCES AT WITS. HE WAS BEFRIENDED BY STUDENTS FROM OTHER RACE GROUPS LIKE RUTH FIRST, GEORGE BIZOS, J N SINGH AND ISMAIL MEER.

LET'S GO GET SOME LUNCH AT MY FLAT.

INDIANS COULD USE THE TRAMS BUT AFRICANS COULD NOT DUE TO SEGREGATION RULES.

YOU ARE NOT ALLOWED TO CARRY A KAFFIR*!

THEY WERE CHARGED WITH INTERFERING WITH THE TRANSPORT SERVICE. BRAM FISCHER, A COMMUNIST PARTY MEMBER, REPRESENTED THEM. FISCHER'S FATHER WAS THE JUDGE PRESIDENT IN THE FREE STATE. THE CASE WAS DISMISSED.

WHAT DO YOU MEAN? DO YOU KNOW THE MEANING OF THAT WORD?

I WILL HAVE YOU ARRESTED AT THE NEXT STOP!

WE WERE LUCKY. THANK GOODNESS THE MAGISTRATE WAS SUCH AN ADMIRER OF BRAM'S FATHER.

* RACIST TERM FOR AFRICAN

THIS IS MADNESS! THE STRIKE WAS NON-VIOLENT, THEY WERE ASKING FOR A LIVING WAGE... NINE PEOPLE WERE KILLED.

Daily Mail

The communists, Rusty Bernstein, JB Marks, and Moses Kotane were arrested in connection with the strike. "Their wild speeches and absurd demands could no longer be tolerated," a spokesman said. Dr. Yusuf Dadoo from the TIC has also been arrested for his role in the strike.

70000 downed tools. "How can such people know anything of trade union procedure."

IN 1948 MAKAZIWE WAS BORN. SHE WAS A FRAIL AND SICKLY BABY.

DESPITE TIRELESS CARE, MAKAZIWE DIED AT ONLY NINE MONTHS.

I'M TRYING FOR A LOAN. AND ONCE I FINISH MY LAW STUDIES, I WILL BRING IN A REASONABLE INCOME.

NELSON, WE CAN BARELY MAKE ENDS MEET... WHAT WILL WE DO...

I JUST WISH I KNEW WHAT IS WRONG WITH HER...

GET SOME REST, EVELYN, I WILL TAKE CARE OF HER TONIGHT...

I AM SO SORRY MY LOVE...

LATER THAT YEAR THEY SUFFERED ANOTHER LOSS. ANTON LEMBEDE COLLAPSED AND WAS RUSHED TO HOSPITAL BY SISULU AND MANDELA. HE DIED THAT NIGHT...

THIS DOES NOT MAKE ANY SENSE...HE WAS ONLY 33 YEARS OLD!

AP MDA SUCCEEDED LEMBEDE. HE SUPPORTED OPENING BRANCHES AT PLACES LIKE FORT HARE TO BRING IN NEW RECRUITS.

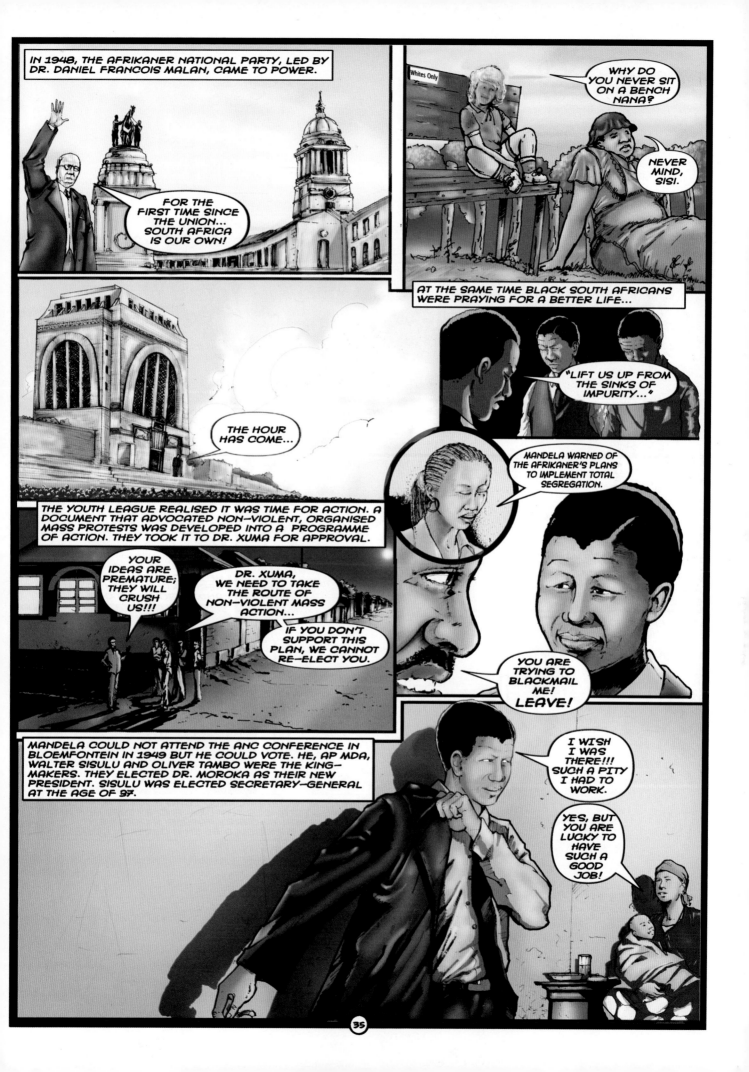

IN 1948, THE AFRIKANER NATIONAL PARTY, LED BY DR. DANIEL FRANCOIS MALAN, CAME TO POWER.

FOR THE FIRST TIME SINCE THE UNION... SOUTH AFRICA IS OUR OWN!

Whites Only

WHY DO YOU NEVER SIT ON A BENCH NANA?

NEVER MIND, SISI.

AT THE SAME TIME BLACK SOUTH AFRICANS WERE PRAYING FOR A BETTER LIFE...

"LIFT US UP FROM THE SINKS OF IMPURITY..."

THE HOUR HAS COME...

MANDELA WARNED OF THE AFRIKANER'S PLANS TO IMPLEMENT TOTAL SEGREGATION.

THE YOUTH LEAGUE REALISED IT WAS TIME FOR ACTION. A DOCUMENT THAT ADVOCATED NON-VIOLENT, ORGANISED MASS PROTESTS WAS DEVELOPED INTO A PROGRAMME OF ACTION. THEY TOOK IT TO DR. XUMA FOR APPROVAL.

YOUR IDEAS ARE PREMATURE; THEY WILL CRUSH US!!!

DR. XUMA, WE NEED TO TAKE THE ROUTE OF NON-VIOLENT MASS ACTION...

IF YOU DON'T SUPPORT THIS PLAN, WE CANNOT RE-ELECT YOU.

YOU ARE TRYING TO BLACKMAIL ME! LEAVE!

MANDELA COULD NOT ATTEND THE ANC CONFERENCE IN BLOEMFONTEIN IN 1949 BUT HE COULD VOTE. HE, AP MDA, WALTER SISULU AND OLIVER TAMBO WERE THE KING-MAKERS. THEY ELECTED DR. MOROKA AS THEIR NEW PRESIDENT. SISULU WAS ELECTED SECRETARY-GENERAL AT THE AGE OF 37.

I WISH I WAS THERE!!! SUCH A PITY I HAD TO WORK.

YES, BUT YOU ARE LUCKY TO HAVE SUCH A GOOD JOB!

MANDELA BEFRIENDED JAZZ LEGENDS LIKE THE MANHATTAN BROTHERS AND TOOK UP BOXING IN A MAKESHIFT GYM IN ORLANDO.

HE ENJOYED DINING AT THE FEW RESTAURANTS OPEN TO AFRICANS, AND HE BOUGHT A CAR...

BUT REPRESSION WAS GROWING...

THIS PASS IS NOT IN ORDER!

HURRY UP!

MOST AFRICANS WORKED LONG HOURS, TRAVELLED LONG DISTANCES TO WORK, AND BY 1952 MEN AND WOMEN HAD TO CARRY PASSES; A DOCUMENT PROVING THEY COULD BE IN A CERTAIN AREA.

BEWARE, LOCK YOUR DOORS AT NIGHT...THE RED MENACE AND BLACK PERIL ARE HERE!

THE SUPPRESSION OF COMMUNISM ACT, UNDER WHICH ACTIVISTS COULD BE BANNED FROM POLITICAL ACTIVITIES, WAS ANNOUNCED.

THE GOVERNMENT BANNED ALL GATHERINGS ON 1 MAY 1950. IN ORLANDO A SMALL PEACEFUL CROWD HAD GATHERED. MANDELA AND SISULU WATCHED FROM THE SIDELINES.

DESPITE THE YOUTH LEAGUE'S OPPOSITION, MORE THAN HALF OF JOHANNESBURG'S WORKERS STAYED AT HOME THAT DAY...

NELSON! THE POLICE ARE HERE. THERE'S TROUBLE COMING!

THE POLICE ANNOUNCED THAT THE PROTESTORS HAD THREE MINUTES TO DISPERSE...

...WITHOUT FURTHER WARNING THEY OPENED FIRE.

MANDELA AND SISULU FOUND SHELTER IN A DORMITORY.

TAKE THAT!

NOOO!!

...OTHERS WERE NOT SO LUCKY...

EIGHTEEN PEOPLE WERE KILLED AND MANY OTHERS WOUNDED IN TOWNSHIPS AROUND THE CITY...

MANDELA AND SISULU HELPED TO TAKE THE INJURED TO HOSPITAL...

I CAN'T BELIEVE WE SURVIVED THAT!

THIS IS A FIERCE ENEMY WE ARE FACING.

THE MAY DAY TRAGEDY STIRRED THE ANC INTO ACTION. IT ASKED OTHER PARTIES TO JOIN IN A NATIONAL DAY OF MOURNING — A STAY-AWAY ON THE 26TH JUNE 1950.

YES, WE ARE OPPOSING THE SUPPRESSION OF COMMUNISM ACT! WE ARE MOURNING FOR OUR BROTHERS AND SISTERS...

NELSON, EVELYN NEEDS YOU...

MAKGATHO LEWANIKA WAS BORN. HE WAS NAMED AFTER SEFAKO MAPOGO MAKGATHO, THE SECOND ANC PRESIDENT. TO MANDELA HIS NAME WAS A SYMBOL OF COURAGE.

POLITICS WAS CAUSING MORE AND MORE FRICTION IN THE MANDELA HOME...

I WISH WE COULD GO BACK TO THE TRANSKEI... THEN WE WOULD SEE MORE OF YOU!

I'M SORRY EVELYN, BUT POLITICS IS NOT A DISTRACTION. IT IS MY LIFE WORK!

JOE SLOVO, A COMMUNIST, TRIED TO CONVINCE THE ANC TO WORK WITH OTHER ORGANISATIONS IN A UNITED FRONT...

WE ARE GETTING THERE, JOE.

DAYS BEFORE IT STARTED MANDELA SPOKE ALONGSIDE ANC NATAL PRESIDENT, CHIEF ALBERT LUTHULI AND DR NAICKER, PRESIDENT OF THE NATAL INDIAN CONGRESS.

WE WELCOME ALL TRUE-HEARTED VOLUNTEERS FROM ALL WALKS OF LIFE, WITHOUT THE CONSIDERATION OF COLOUR, RACE OR CREED...TO DEFY THESE UNJUST LAWS...

"I DO HEREBY PLEDGE TO BIND MYSELF TO SERVE MY COUNTRY AND MY PEOPLE... TO PARTICIPATE FULLY AND WITHOUT RESERVATIONS, TO THE BEST OF MY ABILITY..."

WHITES ONLY
SLEGS BLANKES
TICKET OFFICE

"AFRIKA! MAYIBUYE... LET AFRICA COME BACK!"

26 JUNE 1952, PORT ELIZABETH RAILWAY STATION. RAYMOND MHLABA LED VOLUNTEERS THROUGH A WHITES ONLY ENTRANCE...

ON THE SAME DAY IN BOKSBURG: SISULU AND NANA SITA LED VOLUNTEERS INTO A TOWNSHIP WITHOUT PERMITS.

"THINA SIZWE! GIVE US BACK OUR LAND!"

IF YOU ENTER, YOU WILL ALL BE ARRESTED!

WHITES ONLY

THE VOLUNTEERS WERE ORDERLY AND WELCOMED ARREST.

OPEN UP THE JAILS, MALAN! WE ARE KNOCKING!

WHAT ARE THESE PEOPLE UP TO?

WHITES ONLY TOILETS

MORE THAN 80 000 PEOPLE WERE ARRESTED IN SIX MONTHS. EVEN THOUGH DEFIERS COULD PAY A FINE, THEY REFUSED AND SERVED TIME IN JAIL.

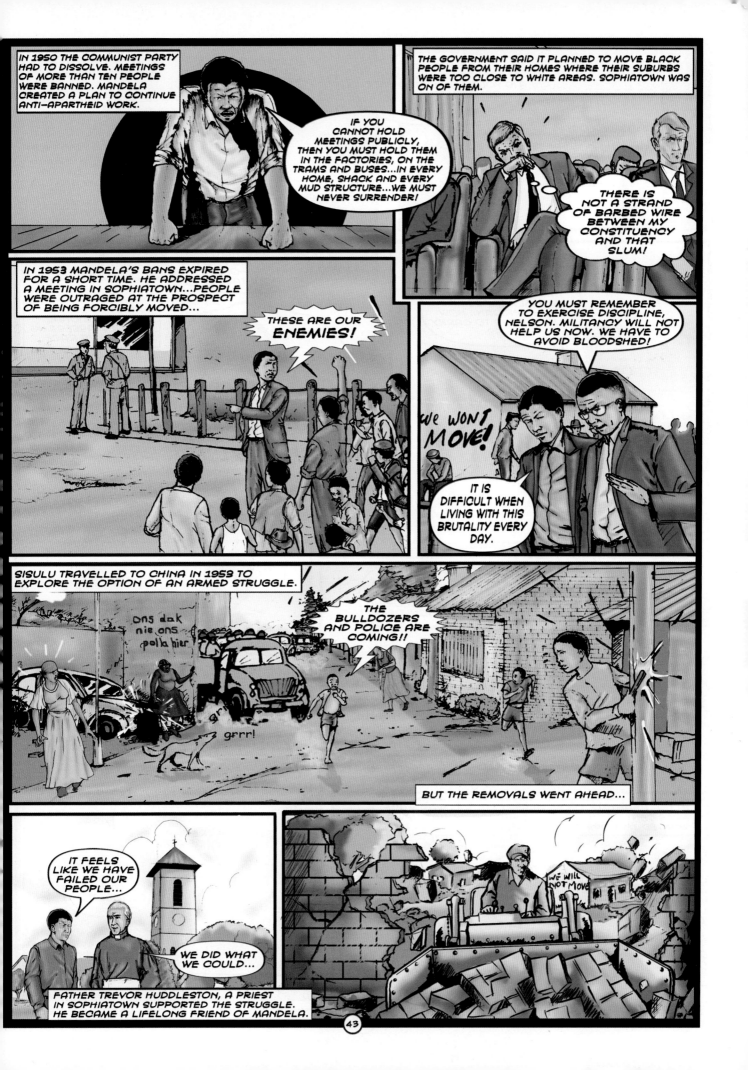

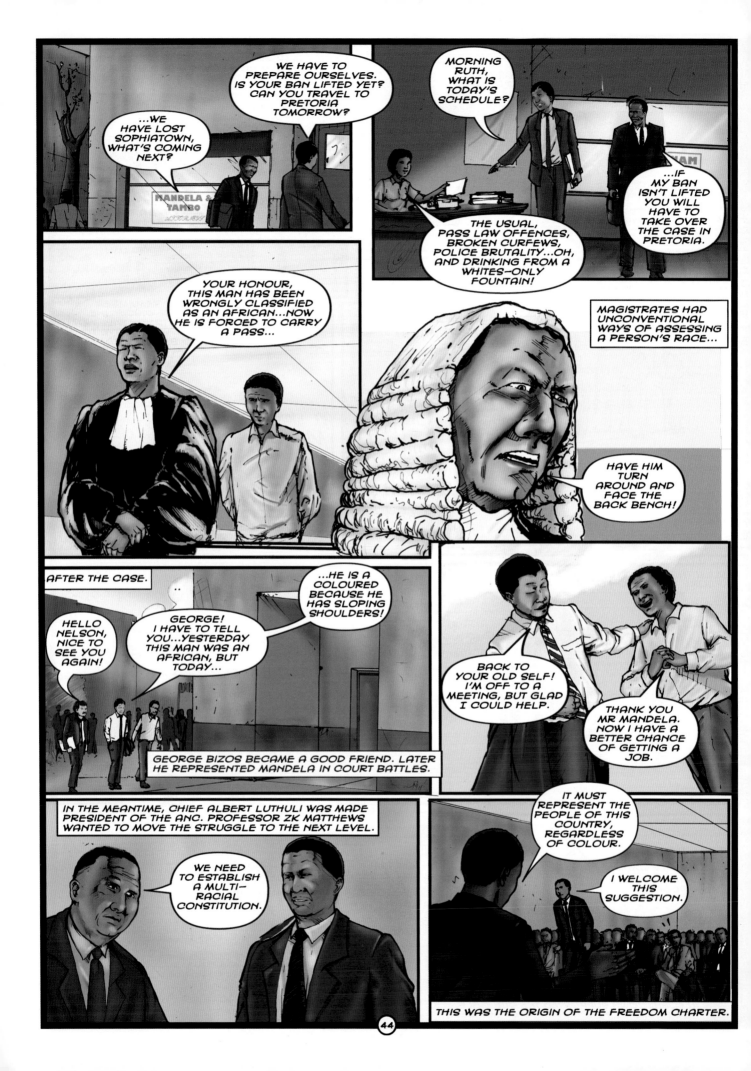

THE ANC, INDIAN CONGRESS, COLOURED PEOPLE'S ORGANISATION AND THE CONGRESS OF DEMOCRATS FORMED THE CONGRESS ALLIANCE AND COLLECTED VIEWS FROM PEOPLE ACROSS THE COUNTRY.

THIS CHAP WANTS TO HAVE PERMISSION TO HAVE 10 WIVES!

I'LL VOTE AGAINST THAT!

WE THE PEOPLE OF SOUTH AFRICA, DECLARE FOR ALL OUR COUNTRY AND THE WORLD TO KNOW THAT SOUTH AFRICA BELONGS TO ALL WHO LIVE IN IT, BLACK AND WHITE AND THAT NO GOVERNMENT CAN JUSTLY CLAIM AUTHORITY UNLESS IT IS BASED ON THE WILL OF THE PEOPLE.

THE FREEDOM CHARTER WAS ADOPTED BY THOUSANDS WHO ATTENDED THE CONGRESS OF THE PEOPLE IN KLIPTOWN.

MANDELA WATCHED FROM A DISTANCE BECAUSE HE WAS BANNED.

WE ARE INVESTIGATING A CASE OF TREASON, DO NOT LEAVE UNTIL WE HAVE YOUR NAME AND YOU HAVE BEEN SEARCHED!

EVERYONE WAS CHECKED BY THE POLICE.

WHILE THE AFRIKANERS ARE ENFORCING THEIR EXCLUSIVE POWER OVER ALL OTHER RACES, WE HAVE DECLARED ALL PEOPLE EQUAL!

YOU NO LONGER SPEND ANY TIME AT HOME...

I CANNOT BE PASSIVE IN THE FACE OF OPPRESSION!

YOU SHOULD SERVE GOD!

BY NOW THE COUPLE HAD ANOTHER BABY GIRL. THEY NAMED HER MAKAZIWE, TO HONOUR HER SISTER WHO DIED, BUT THEIR MARRIAGE WAS IN TROUBLE...

I MUST GO AND VISIT MY FAMILY.

MANDELA'S SECOND BAN EXPIRED AND HE TOOK THE OPPORTUNITY TO LEAVE JOHANNESBURG TO SEE HIS FAMILY IN THE TRANSKEI AND TO ORGANISE FOR THE ANC.

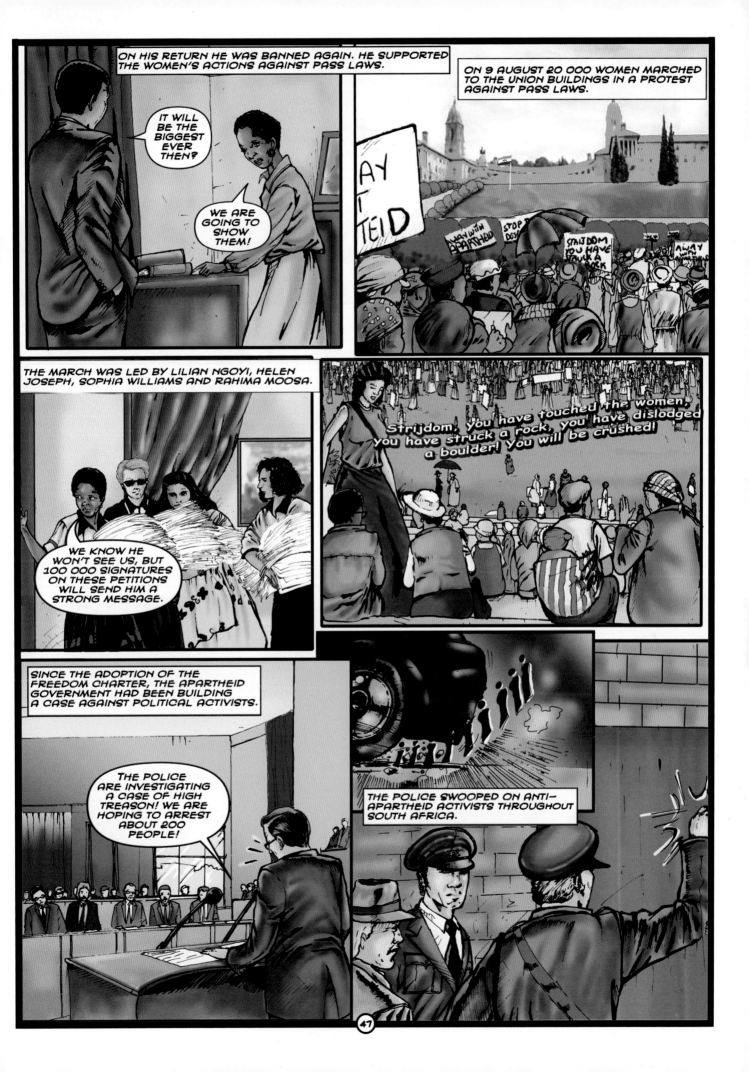

3 THE BLACK PIMPERNEL

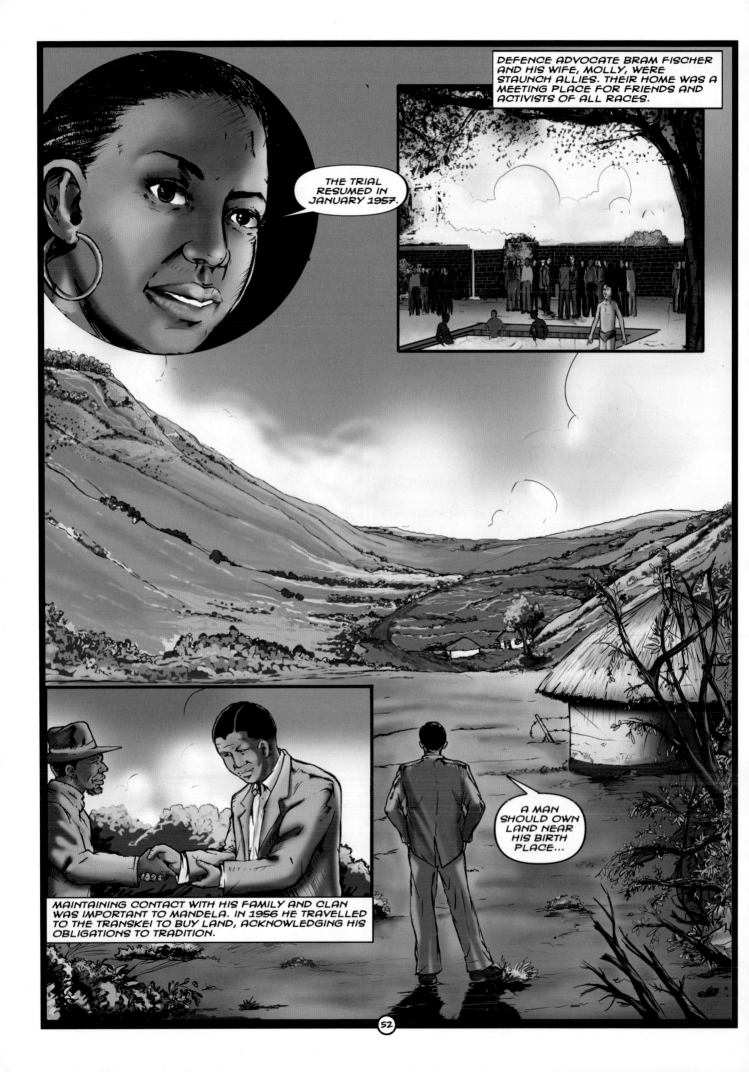

THE TRIAL RESUMED IN JANUARY 1957.

DEFENCE ADVOCATE BRAM FISCHER AND HIS WIFE, MOLLY, WERE STAUNCH ALLIES. THEIR HOME WAS A MEETING PLACE FOR FRIENDS AND ACTIVISTS OF ALL RACES.

A MAN SHOULD OWN LAND NEAR HIS BIRTH PLACE...

MAINTAINING CONTACT WITH HIS FAMILY AND CLAN WAS IMPORTANT TO MANDELA. IN 1956 HE TRAVELLED TO THE TRANSKEI TO BUY LAND, ACKNOWLEDGING HIS OBLIGATIONS TO TRADITION.

IN APRIL 1958 THE ANC AND ITS CONGRESS ALLIANCE PARTNERS PLANNED A 3-DAY STAY AWAY TO PROTEST AGAINST THE WHITES ONLY ELECTION.

THE BUSES ARE FULL... THE PEOPLE ARE GOING TO WORK!

THE AFRICANISTS HAVE NOT SUPPORTED OUR STRIKE. THEY JUST CANNOT SEE THAT WE NEED TO COMBINE FORCES WITH PEOPLE FROM OTHER RACE GROUPS.

BUT IN SOPHIATOWN, THE STRIKE CONTINUED FOR A FULL THREE DAYS. THE POLICE RAIDED HOMES AND FORCED RESIDENTS TO GO TO WORK...

IN AUGUST 1958 THE TREASON TRIAL RESUMED. THREE JUDGES RULED LATER THAT YEAR THAT THE CHARGES BE WITHDRAWN. WITHIN A MONTH 30 OF THE TRIALISTS WERE CHARGED AGAIN!

THE TRANSVAAL ANC HELD A CRISIS CONFERENCE IN NOVEMBER 1958. THE SPLIT BETWEEN THE AFRICANISTS AND OTHER MEMBERS WAS CAUSING DIVISION IN THE MOVEMENT.

IT'S SOBUKWE'S TURN TO SPEAK...

WHITES CAN NEVER FULLY IDENTIFY WITH THE BLACK CAUSE... WE NEED A GOVERNMENT OF THE AFRICANS, BY THE AFRICANS AND FOR THE AFRICANS!

LET US WHO DISAGREE WITH THE EXECUTIVE'S POLICIES LEAVE NOW!

56

ON 31 MARCH 1960 A STATE OF EMERGENCY WAS DECLARED, GIVING THE GOVERNMENT SWEEPING POWERS TO CRUSH ALL OPPOSITION.

WHERE ARE YOUR WARRANTS? WHERE ARE YOU TAKING HIM?

MIND YOUR OWN BUSINESS!

MANDELA WAS TAKEN TO NEWLANDS POLICE STATION NEAR SOPHIATOWN... THE COURTYARD WAS SO CROWDED THEY COULD NOT EVEN SIT DOWN.

BE QUIET OR YOU WILL BE SORRY, BOY!

WE NEED FOOD AND WATER!

THEY WERE GIVEN A THIN MAIZE LIQUID TO EAT AND BLOOD-STAINED BLANKETS COVERED IN LICE AND COCKROACHES.

THE NEXT NIGHT THEY WERE RELEASED...

BANG

...FOR A FEW SECONDS, AND THEN FORMALLY ARRESTED UNDER EMERGENCY REGULATIONS.

MANDELA AND OTHERS WERE TRANSFERRED TO PRETORIA LOCAL PRISON.

ON 8 APRIL 1960 THE ANC AND PAC WERE BANNED.

WE CANNOT DEFEND YOU FAIRLY UNDER THE EMERGENCY LAWS!

I AGREE WITH YOU BRAM..

THE LAWYERS WITHDREW FROM THE CASE ...

IN DECEMBER 1960 MANDELA RECEIVED NEWS THAT HIS SON, MAKGATHO, HAD FALLEN ILL IN THE TRANSKEI.

WHAT ABOUT YOUR BANNING ORDER?

LET THEM ARREST ME FOR GOING TO SEE MY SON!

HE DROVE THROUGH THE NIGHT. MAKGATHO WAS BEING CARED FOR BY MATANZIMA'S WIFE.

I MUST GET HIM TO A HOSPITAL IN JOBURG.

DRIVE CAREFULLY MADIBA!

HE WILL BE FINE... NOW I HAVE TO GO TO WINNIE.

GO NOW.

DURING HIS DASH TO THE TRANSKEI, THEIR SECOND DAUGHTER, ZINDZISWA, WAS BORN.

MANDELA'S PROFILE AS AN ANC NATIONAL LEADER MEANT THAT HE OFTEN TRAVELLED.

WINNIE, THE TRIAL IS ADJOURNED. BUT I WILL SOON BE ATTENDING THE CONFERENCE.

LIFE WITH YOU IS LIKE LIFE WITHOUT YOU...

I MUST GO TO EVELYN'S TO SAY GOODBYE TO MAKGATHO AND MAKI BEFORE I GO UNDERGROUND. I WON'T BE ABLE TO SEE THEMBI. HE IS IN THE TRANSKEI.

MANDELA LEFT FOR PIETERMARITZBURG, KNOWING THAT HE WOULD GO INTO HIDING AS SOON AS THE TREASON TRIAL ENDED.

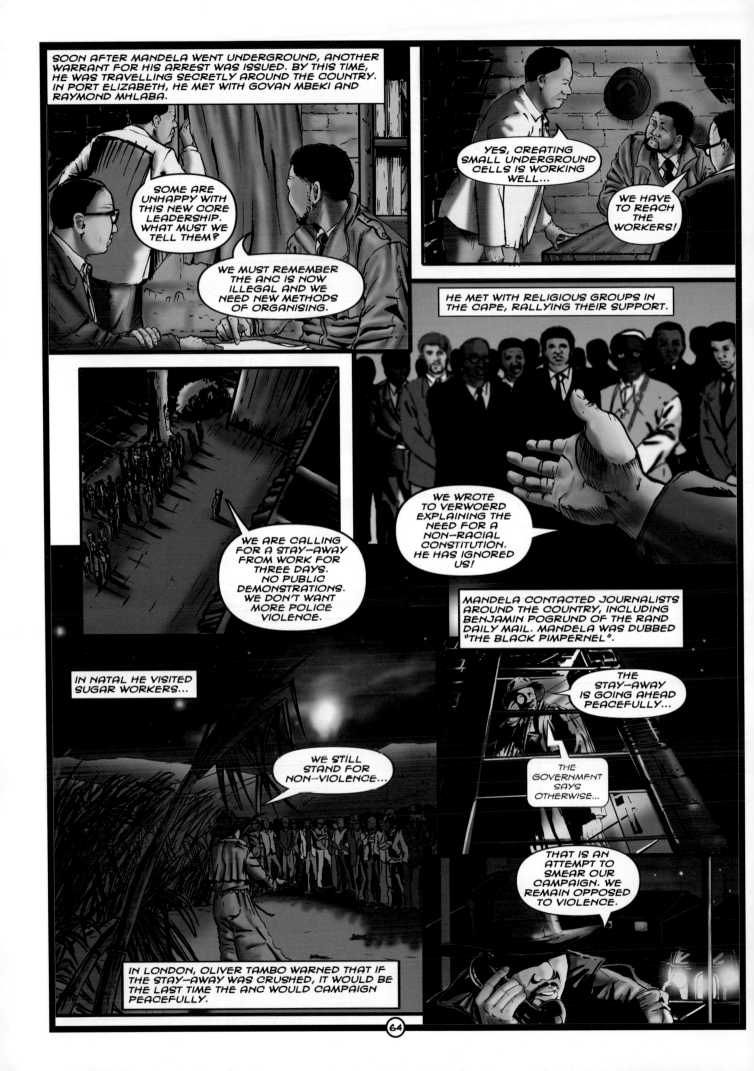

SOON AFTER MANDELA WENT UNDERGROUND, ANOTHER WARRANT FOR HIS ARREST WAS ISSUED. BY THIS TIME, HE WAS TRAVELLING SECRETLY AROUND THE COUNTRY. IN PORT ELIZABETH, HE MET WITH GOVAN MBEKI AND RAYMOND MHLABA.

SOME ARE UNHAPPY WITH THIS NEW CORE LEADERSHIP. WHAT MUST WE TELL THEM?

WE MUST REMEMBER THE ANC IS NOW ILLEGAL AND WE NEED NEW METHODS OF ORGANISING.

YES, CREATING SMALL UNDERGROUND CELLS IS WORKING WELL...

WE HAVE TO REACH THE WORKERS!

HE MET WITH RELIGIOUS GROUPS IN THE CAPE, RALLYING THEIR SUPPORT.

WE ARE CALLING FOR A STAY-AWAY FROM WORK FOR THREE DAYS. NO PUBLIC DEMONSTRATIONS. WE DON'T WANT MORE POLICE VIOLENCE.

WE WROTE TO VERWOERD EXPLAINING THE NEED FOR A NON-RACIAL CONSTITUTION. HE HAS IGNORED US!

MANDELA CONTACTED JOURNALISTS AROUND THE COUNTRY, INCLUDING BENJAMIN POGRUND OF THE RAND DAILY MAIL. MANDELA WAS DUBBED "THE BLACK PIMPERNEL".

IN NATAL HE VISITED SUGAR WORKERS...

WE STILL STAND FOR NON-VIOLENCE...

THE STAY-AWAY IS GOING AHEAD PEACEFULLY...

THE GOVERNMENT SAYS OTHERWISE...

THAT IS AN ATTEMPT TO SMEAR OUR CAMPAIGN. WE REMAIN OPPOSED TO VIOLENCE.

IN LONDON, OLIVER TAMBO WARNED THAT IF THE STAY-AWAY WAS CRUSHED, IT WOULD BE THE LAST TIME THE ANC WOULD CAMPAIGN PEACEFULLY.

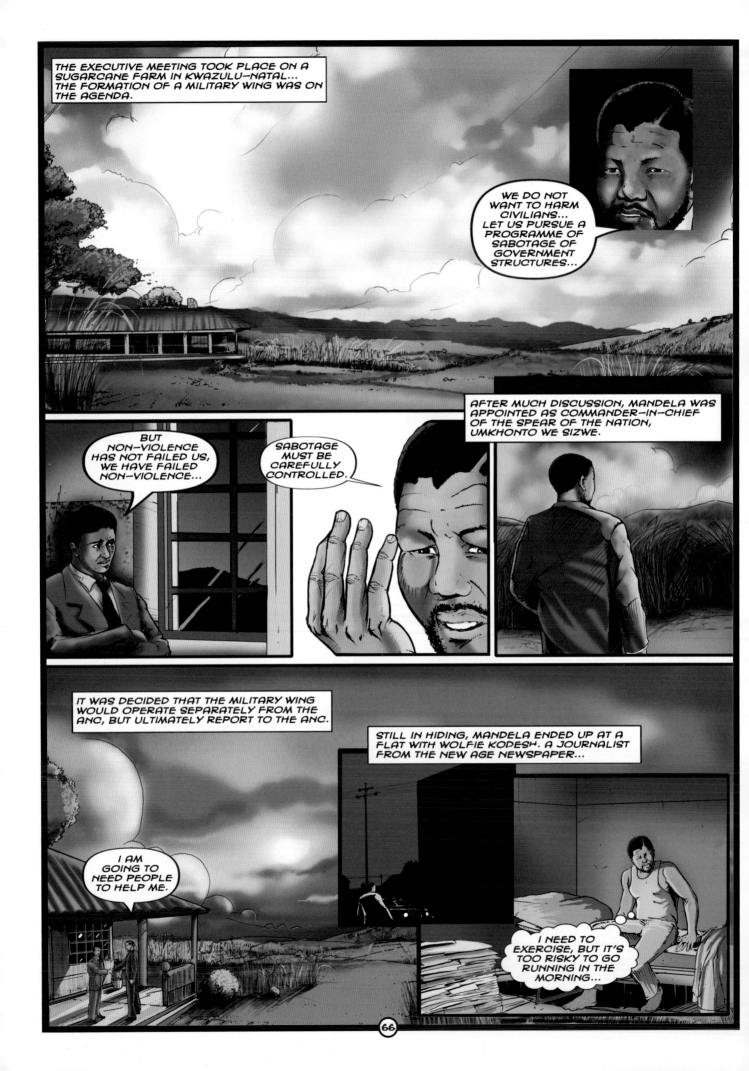

THE EXECUTIVE MEETING TOOK PLACE ON A SUGARCANE FARM IN KWAZULU-NATAL... THE FORMATION OF A MILITARY WING WAS ON THE AGENDA.

WE DO NOT WANT TO HARM CIVILIANS... LET US PURSUE A PROGRAMME OF SABOTAGE OF GOVERNMENT STRUCTURES...

AFTER MUCH DISCUSSION, MANDELA WAS APPOINTED AS COMMANDER-IN-CHIEF OF THE SPEAR OF THE NATION, UMKHONTO WE SIZWE.

BUT NON-VIOLENCE HAS NOT FAILED US, WE HAVE FAILED NON-VIOLENCE...

SABOTAGE MUST BE CAREFULLY CONTROLLED.

IT WAS DECIDED THAT THE MILITARY WING WOULD OPERATE SEPARATELY FROM THE ANC, BUT ULTIMATELY REPORT TO THE ANC.

STILL IN HIDING, MANDELA ENDED UP AT A FLAT WITH WOLFIE KODESH, A JOURNALIST FROM THE NEW AGE NEWSPAPER...

I AM GOING TO NEED PEOPLE TO HELP ME.

I NEED TO EXERCISE, BUT IT'S TOO RISKY TO GO RUNNING IN THE MORNING...

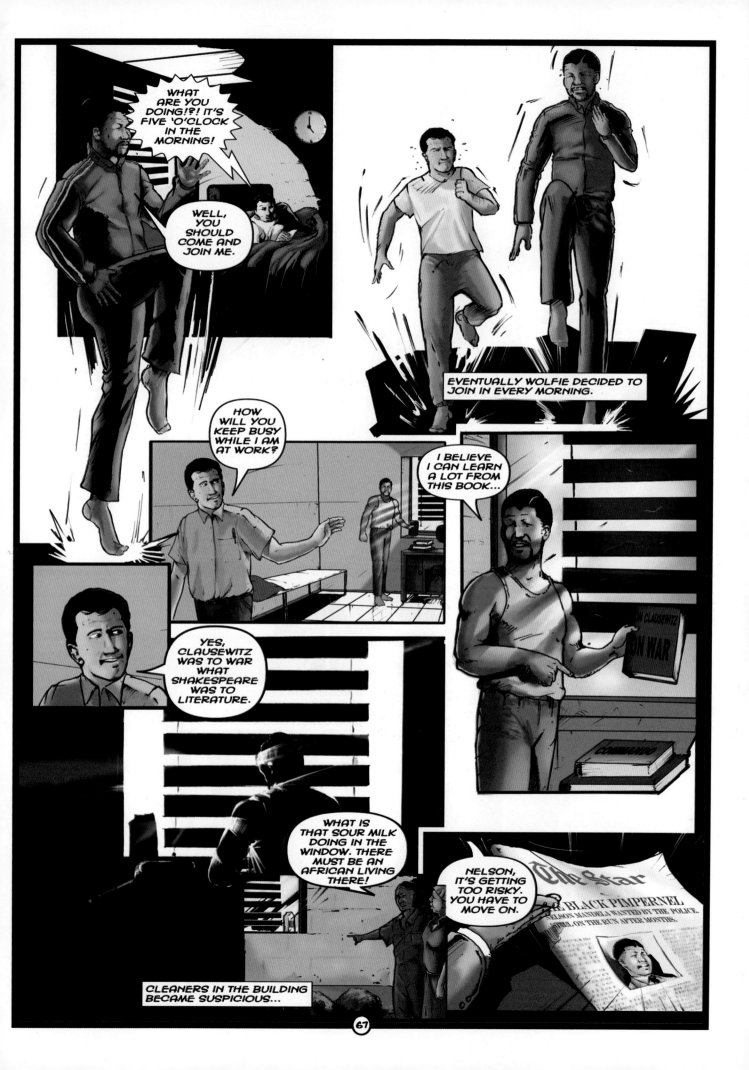

WHEN ARE YOU COMING HOME?

MANDELA POSED AS A GARDENER ON THE PROPERTY.

...BUT ALSO ATTENDED MEETINGS.

HELLO.

JOE SLOVO AND JACK HODGSON, WHO HAD SERVED IN WORLD WAR TWO, WERE AMONGST THOSE MANDELA MET WITH...

JACK HAS COME TO HELP US WITH SOME IDEAS FOR SABOTAGE.

NOW, IF WE TARGET THESE KEY AREAS, WE CAN DAMAGE THE LINKS BETWEEN MAJOR CENTRES IN THE COUNTRY...

YES, I SEE! MINIMUM MANPOWER, MAXIMUM EFFECT...

THE ANC WAS INVITED TO ATTEND THE PAN-AFRICAN FREEDOM MOVEMENT FOR EAST, CENTRAL AND SOUTHERN AFRICA CONFERENCE IN ADDIS ABABA, ETHIOPIA. MANDELA WAS ASKED TO REPRESENT THE ANC.

CHIEF LUTHULI, I WILL BE LEAVING SOON. I WILL NEED ALL THE SUPPORT I CAN GET.

BUT OF COURSE. WE NEED A STRONG LEADER TO REPRESENT US IN AFRICA!

I DON'T KNOW WHEN I WILL RETURN.

THE JOURNEY BEGAN WITH A TRIP OUT OF THE COUNTRY, TO BECHUANALAND (BOTSWANA) IN JANUARY 1962...

WHAT LIES AHEAD? WILL THE BLACK PIMPERNEL RETURN?

4

THE TRIALIST

MANDELA: TO LIVE OR DIE ?

THIS IS THE PALACE OF JUSTICE – THE HIGH COURT – WHERE THE RIVONIA TRIAL TOOK PLACE.

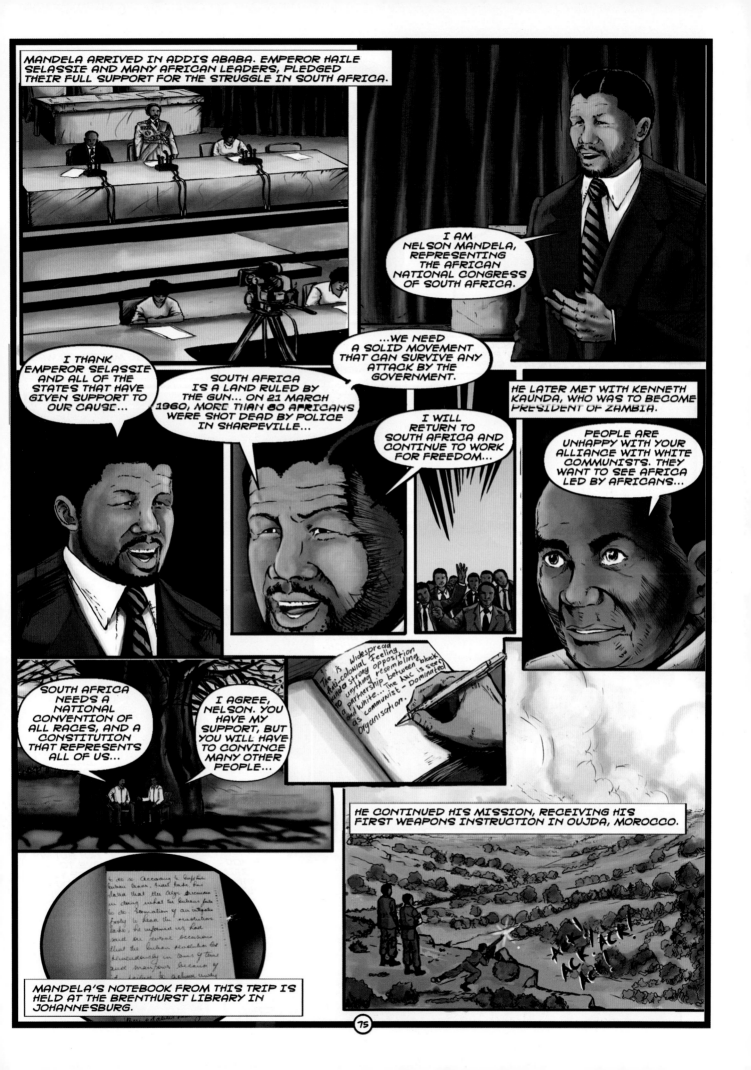

IN SENEGAL, HE AND TAMBO MET WITH PRESIDENT LEOPOLD SENGHOR.

YOU'RE SICK, OLIVER, WE SHOULD GET YOU BACK TO THE HOTEL...

NO, THE MEETING IS TOO IMPORTANT...

I WILL CARRY YOU!

COUGH!! COUGH!! COUGH!!

WE HAVE GREAT RESPECT FOR CHIEF LUTHULI. WE WILL DO ALL WE CAN TO ASSIST...

AS SOON AS TAMBO WAS FIT ENOUGH, THEY TRAVELLED TO LONDON TO MEET POLITICIANS, JOURNALISTS, ACTIVISTS AND SUPPORTERS.

ONE OF THESE MEETINGS WAS WITH CANON JOHN COLLINS...

IT'S GOOD TO SEE YOU, NELSON.

WE COULD NOT HAVE CONTINUED WITHOUT YOUR SUPPORT...

WE WILL SEE TODD AND ESME MATSHIKIZA.

TODD, A JOURNALIST AND COMPOSER OF THE MUSICAL HIT, KING KONG, AND HIS WIFE LIVED IN EXILE IN LONDON...

WHY GO BACK TO SUCH A LIFE, NELSON?

THE POLICE HAVE BEEN HUNTING ME FOR TEN MONTHS NOW...

I NEED TO BE PART OF THE STRUGGLE BACK HOME...

BEFORE LEAVING LONDON, MANDELA MET WITH OLD FRIEND AND INDIAN CONGRESS LEADER, YUSUF DADOO...

OUR POLICY OF MULTI-RACIALISM IS NOT ACCEPTED BY MANY LEADERS IN AFRICA. WE HAVE TO CHANGE OUR IMAGE!

ARE YOU SUGGESTING WE CHANGE OUR POLICY?!?

NO! BUT WE HAVE TO TAKE THESE VIEWS SERIOUSLY, AND PERHAPS EVEN CHANGE THE PUBLIC FACE OF THE ANC...

76

SURROUNDED, HE CONTEMPLATED AN ESCAPE, BUT WAS QUICKLY APPROACHED BY THE POLICE...

NAME?

DAVID MOTSAMAYI.

WE KNOW YOU ARE NELSON MANDELA!

THE "BLACK PIMPERNEL" HAD EVADED CAPTURE FOR 17 MONTHS...

IT'S TOO SOON!

HE WAS TRANSFERRED TO A PRISON IN JOHANNESBURG WHERE HE WAS ALLOWED TO CONSULT WITH JOE SLOVO, A LAWYER AND FRIEND.

THE FREE MANDELA COMMITTEE WAS SET UP, WITH KATHRADA AS ITS SECRETARY. PROTESTS WERE HELD AROUND THE COUNTRY.

PLEASE ENSURE MY NOTEBOOKS AT LILIESLEAF HAVE BEEN REMOVED.

I'VE BEEN TOLD THAT THEY HAVE...

I WILL CONDUCT MY OWN DEFENCE, BUT I WILL NEED YOU, JOE...

NO MORE CHAINS

we want to free fro

FREE MANDELA.

FREE US!

MANDELA IS IN PRISON the PEOPLE ARE IN CHAINS

Prison!

IN PRISON MANDELA REGISTERED FOR A LAW DEGREE THROUGH THE UNIVERSITY OF LONDON.

HOW ARE YOU AND THE CHILDREN DOING, WINNIE?

THINGS ARE DIFFICULT, BRAM, BUT WE'RE COPING.

CONDITIONS WERE TOUGH FOR WINNIE AND BRAM FISCHER ADVISED HER TO LEAVE THE COUNTRY.

BUT HER COMMITMENT TO THE STRUGGLE WAS STRONG. SHE WAS INVITED TO SPEAK TO THE INDIAN YOUTH CONGRESS.

I SPEAK FOR MY HUSBAND, WHO CANNOT BE HERE...

I AM VERY PROUD OF YOU!

YOU HAVE BEEN ELECTED AS HONORARY PRESIDENT OF THE INDIAN YOUTH CONGRESS!

THE OLD FORT STILL STANDS IN JOHANNESBURG AND HAS BEEN TURNED INTO A MUSEUM.

WINNIE WENT TO THE OLD FORT TO VISIT HIM.

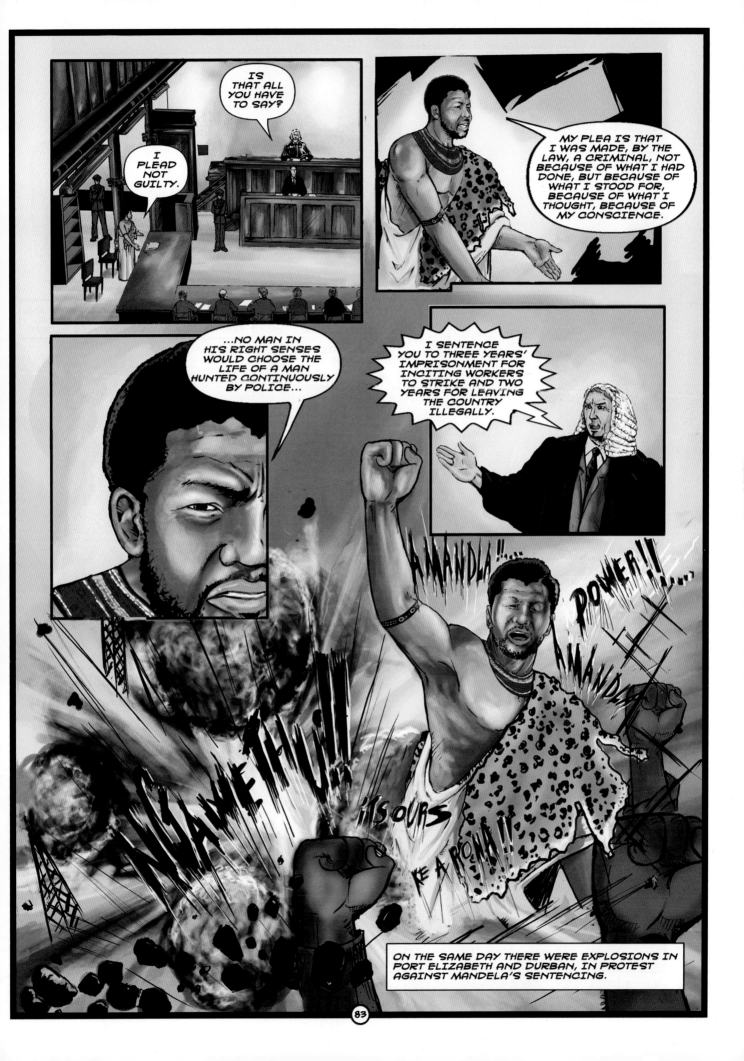

IS THAT ALL YOU HAVE TO SAY?

I PLEAD NOT GUILTY.

MY PLEA IS THAT I WAS MADE, BY THE LAW, A CRIMINAL, NOT BECAUSE OF WHAT I HAD DONE, BUT BECAUSE OF WHAT I STOOD FOR, BECAUSE OF WHAT I THOUGHT, BECAUSE OF MY CONSCIENCE.

...NO MAN IN HIS RIGHT SENSES WOULD CHOOSE THE LIFE OF A MAN HUNTED CONTINUOUSLY BY POLICE...

I SENTENCE YOU TO THREE YEARS' IMPRISONMENT FOR INCITING WORKERS TO STRIKE AND TWO YEARS FOR LEAVING THE COUNTRY ILLEGALLY.

AMANDLA!!

POWER!!

NGAWETHU!!

IT'S OURS

KE A RONA!!

ON THE SAME DAY THERE WERE EXPLOSIONS IN PORT ELIZABETH AND DURBAN, IN PROTEST AGAINST MANDELA'S SENTENCING.

MANDELA WAS TRANSFERRED BACK TO PRETORIA UNAWARE OF THE ARRESTS AT LILIESLEAF. HE WAS ISOLATED IN A SINGLE CELL. HIS TRAVEL DIARY AND MANY DOCUMENTS IN HIS HANDWRITING WERE SEIZED AT THE FARM – THE DOCUMENTS HAD NOT BEEN REMOVED AS HE HAD REQUESTED.

THOMAS MASHIFANE!?!

IF THEY GOT THOMAS, THEY MUST HAVE GOT TO LILIESLEAF!

WALTER SISULU

LIONEL BERNSTEIN

DENIS GOLDBERG

ELIAS MOTSOALEDI

GOVAN MBEKI

ANDREW MLANGENI

AHMED KATHRADA

RAYMOND MHLABA

THOSE ARRESTED AT LILIESLEAF WERE DETAINED AT PRETORIA PRISON UNDER THE NINETY-DAY DETENTION LAW... MOOSA MOOLA, ABDULHAY JASSAT, HAROLD WOLPE AND ARTHUR GOLDREICH, WHO WERE HELD AT MARSHALL SQUARE POLICE STATION, MANAGED TO ESCAPE...

THE MEN WERE CHARGED WITH SABOTAGE... A DAY LATER THEY WERE FINALLY ALLOWED TO SEE EACH OTHER AND THE LAWYERS THEIR FAMILIES HAD ORGANISED.

NELSON! YOU'VE LOST WEIGHT!

IT IS THE COLD PORRIDGE!

THIS IS SERIOUS! THE STATE WILL ASK FOR THE DEATH PENALTY...

THEY WERE TO BE DEFENDED BY BRAM FISCHER, VERNON BERRANGE, JOEL JOFFE, GEORGE BIZOS AND ARTHUR CHASKALSON... BUT JIMMY KANTOR AND BOB HEPPLE'S SITUATIONS WERE NOT SO EASY TO DEAL WITH...

I HAVE TO SEPARATE MY TRIAL FROM THE REST. I AM ONLY HERE BECAUSE MY BROTHER-IN-LAW, WOLPE, ESCAPED!

... AND I HAVE BEEN ASKED TO BE A STATE WITNESS... I AM STILL CONSIDERING WHAT TO DO...

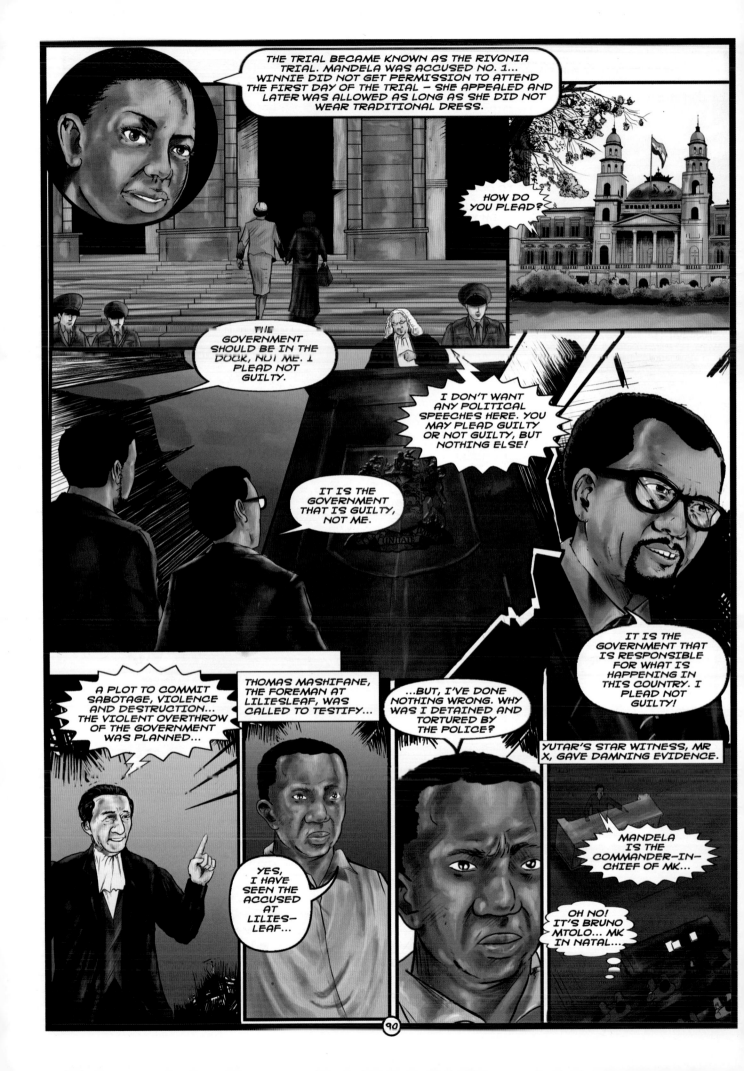

5

PRISONER 466/64

ROBBEN ISLAND IS NOW A WORLD HERITAGE SITE, AND A SYMBOL OF RESISTANCE TO OPPRESSION.

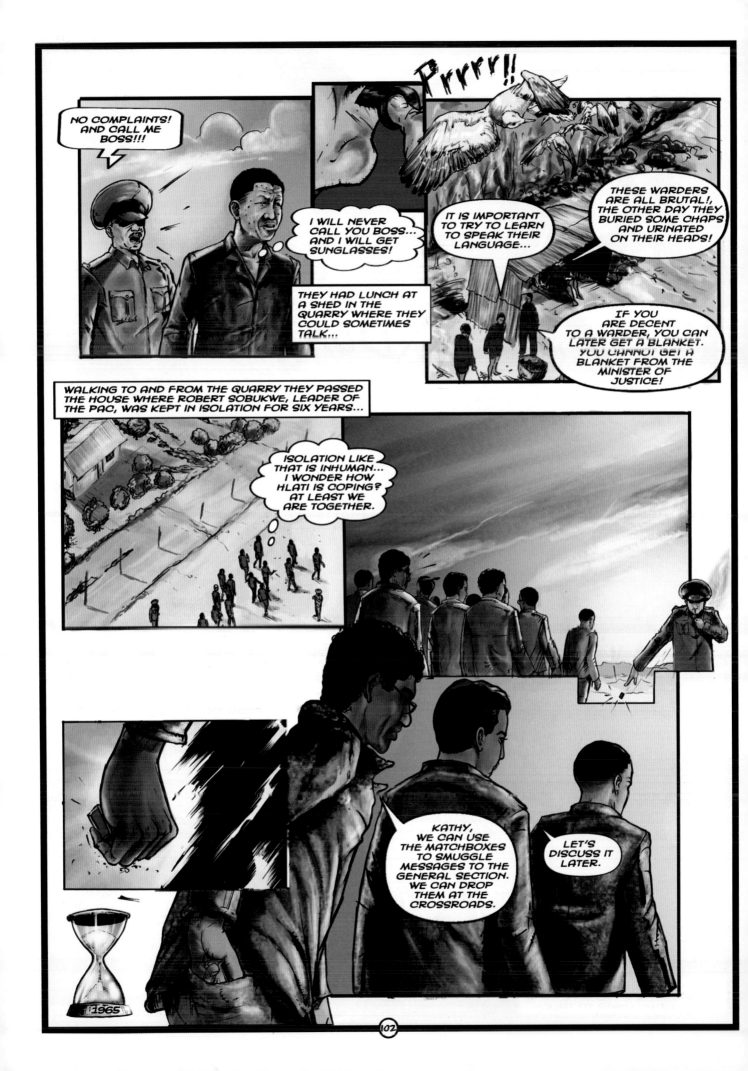

CONTACT BETWEEN THE GENERAL PRISONERS IN COMMUNAL CELLS AND B SECTION WAS STRICTLY FORBIDDEN.

THE HIGH ORGAN SET UP A COMMUNICATIONS COMMITTEE TO FIND WAYS OF MAKING CONTACT.

IT WAS ESSENTIAL TO KEEP IN TOUCH WITH EACH OTHER AND THE OUTSIDE...

IN JULY 1966, A SMUGGLED MESSAGE INFORMED THE PRISONERS OF A HUNGER STRIKE IN THE GENERAL SECTION. SECTION B JOINED IN.

*On hunger strike-general section !!!!

WHY STRIKE? YOU DON'T EVEN KNOW WHY THE OTHERS ARE NOT EATING!

PRISONERS WERE GETTING WEAK FROM LACK OF NOURISHMENT COMBINED WITH HARD LABOUR.

WE SEE ANY ACTION OF PROTEST TO ALTER PRISON CONDITIONS AS PART OF THE STRUGGLE AGAINST APARTHEID.

MANY MEN FROM THE GENERAL SECTION ENDED UP IN HOSPITAL...

COMRADES WILL START DYING SOON!

EVENTUALLY THE AUTHORITIES NEGOTIATED AND THE STRIKE ENDED.

EARLIER IN 1969 MANDELA SENT A PETITION FOR THE RELEASE OF ALL POLITICAL PRISONERS TO THE MINISTER OF JUSTICE.

IN 1970 HE WROTE A LETTER OF COMPLAINT TO THE COMMISSIONER OF PRISONS ABOUT PRISON CONDITIONS.

A BRUTAL NEW COMMANDING OFFICER ARRIVED.

MANDELA AND HIS FRIENDS WON'T LISTEN! HE STILL ACTS AS THEIR REPRESENTATIVE! YOU MUST RESTORE DISCIPLINE!

...LEAVE IT TO ME, WE WILL BREAK THEM!

I HAVE BEEN TELLING YOU TO WORK HARDER BUT YOU WON'T LISTEN! SO I AM REDUCING ALL YOUR CLASSIFICATIONS!

ALL PRISONER COMPLAINTS WERE IGNORED AND SOME WHO REQUESTED TO SEE THEIR LAWYERS WERE PLACED IN SOLITARY CONFINEMENT.

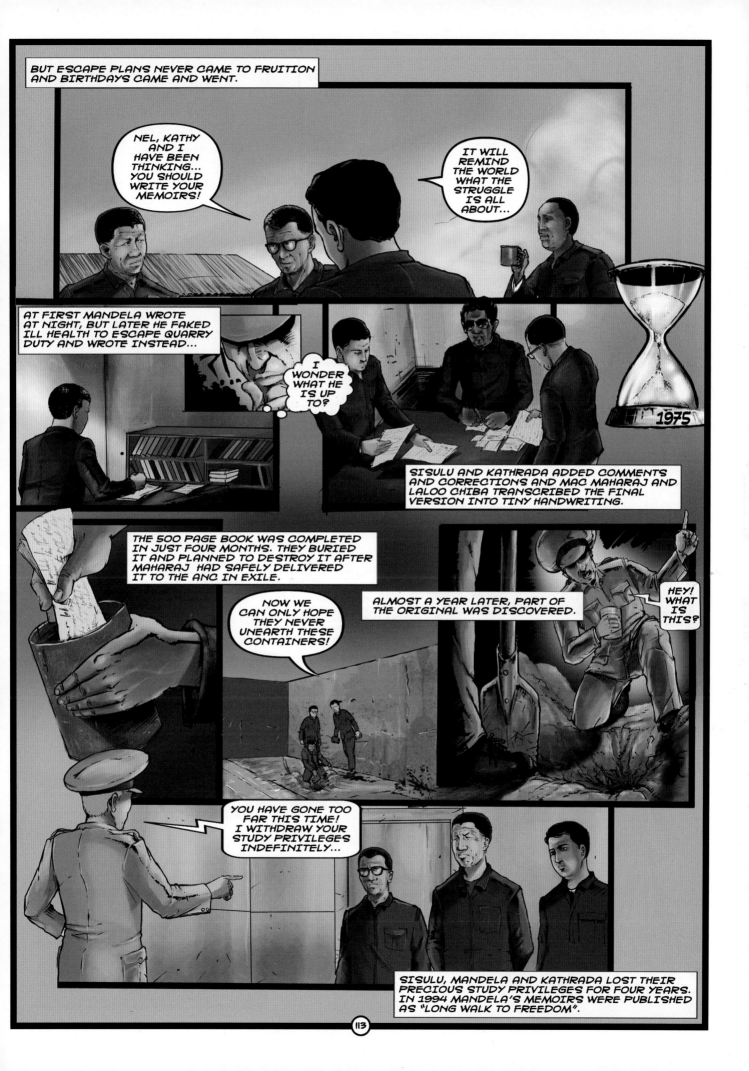

BUT ESCAPE PLANS NEVER CAME TO FRUITION AND BIRTHDAYS CAME AND WENT.

NEL, KATHY AND I HAVE BEEN THINKING... YOU SHOULD WRITE YOUR MEMOIRS!

IT WILL REMIND THE WORLD WHAT THE STRUGGLE IS ALL ABOUT...

AT FIRST MANDELA WROTE AT NIGHT, BUT LATER HE FAKED ILL HEALTH TO ESCAPE QUARRY DUTY AND WROTE INSTEAD...

I WONDER WHAT HE IS UP TO?

1975

SISULU AND KATHRADA ADDED COMMENTS AND CORRECTIONS AND MAC MAHARAJ AND LALOO CHIBA TRANSCRIBED THE FINAL VERSION INTO TINY HANDWRITING.

THE 500 PAGE BOOK WAS COMPLETED IN JUST FOUR MONTHS. THEY BURIED IT AND PLANNED TO DESTROY IT AFTER MAHARAJ HAD SAFELY DELIVERED IT TO THE ANC IN EXILE.

NOW WE CAN ONLY HOPE THEY NEVER UNEARTH THESE CONTAINERS!

ALMOST A YEAR LATER, PART OF THE ORIGINAL WAS DISCOVERED.

HEY! WHAT IS THIS?

YOU HAVE GONE TOO FAR THIS TIME! I WITHDRAW YOUR STUDY PRIVILEGES INDEFINITELY...

SISULU, MANDELA AND KATHRADA LOST THEIR PRECIOUS STUDY PRIVILEGES FOR FOUR YEARS. IN 1994 MANDELA'S MEMOIRS WERE PUBLISHED AS "LONG WALK TO FREEDOM".

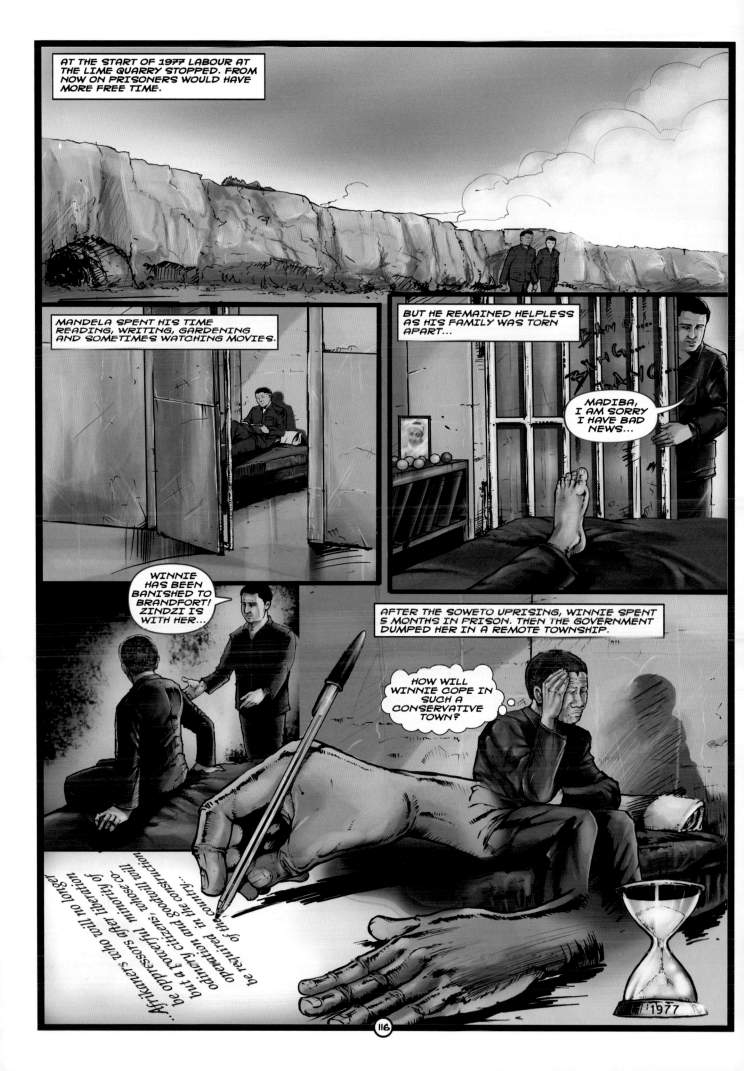

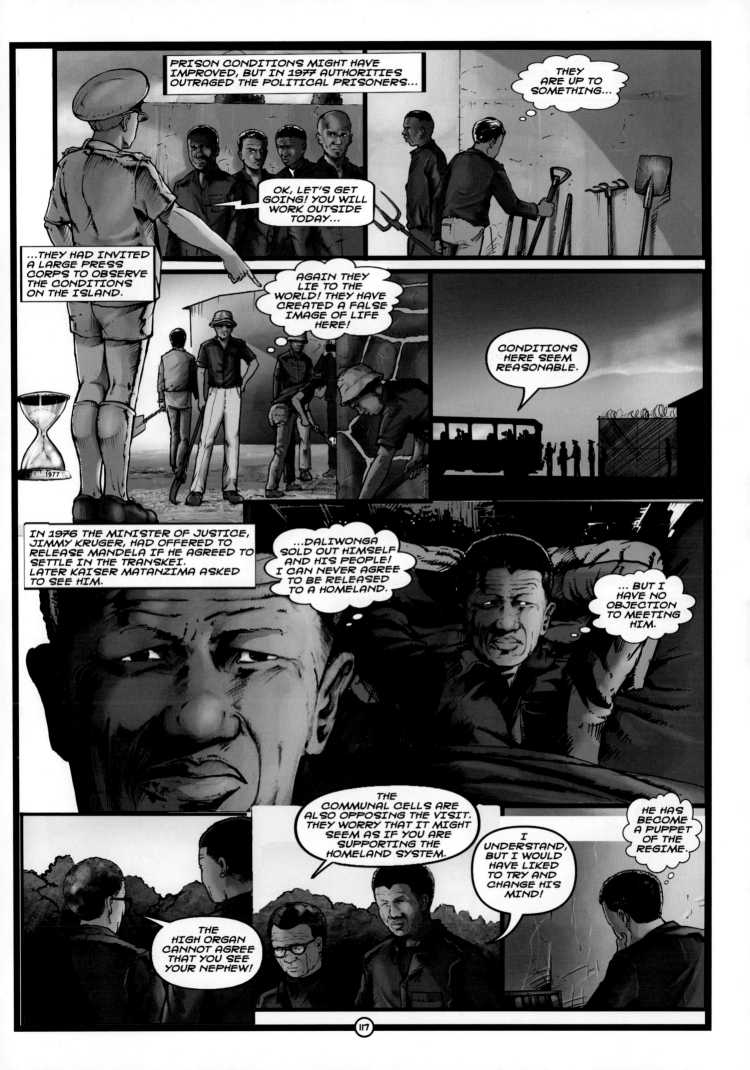

PRISON CONDITIONS MIGHT HAVE IMPROVED, BUT IN 1977 AUTHORITIES OUTRAGED THE POLITICAL PRISONERS...

THEY ARE UP TO SOMETHING...

OK, LET'S GET GOING! YOU WILL WORK OUTSIDE TODAY...

...THEY HAD INVITED A LARGE PRESS CORPS TO OBSERVE THE CONDITIONS ON THE ISLAND.

AGAIN THEY LIE TO THE WORLD! THEY HAVE CREATED A FALSE IMAGE OF LIFE HERE!

CONDITIONS HERE SEEM REASONABLE.

1977

IN 1976 THE MINISTER OF JUSTICE, JIMMY KRUGER, HAD OFFERED TO RELEASE MANDELA IF HE AGREED TO SETTLE IN THE TRANSKEI. LATER KAISER MATANZIMA ASKED TO SEE HIM.

...DALIWONGA SOLD OUT HIMSELF AND HIS PEOPLE! I CAN NEVER AGREE TO BE RELEASED TO A HOMELAND.

... BUT I HAVE NO OBJECTION TO MEETING HIM.

THE COMMUNAL CELLS ARE ALSO OPPOSING THE VISIT. THEY WORRY THAT IT MIGHT SEEM AS IF YOU ARE SUPPORTING THE HOMELAND SYSTEM.

I UNDERSTAND, BUT I WOULD HAVE LIKED TO TRY AND CHANGE HIS MIND!

HE HAS BECOME A PUPPET OF THE REGIME.

THE HIGH ORGAN CANNOT AGREE THAT YOU SEE YOUR NEPHEW!

EACH YEAR CHRISTMAS WAS MARKED WITH THE PRISONERS BEING ALLOWED TO BUY SOME SWEETS AND AN EXTRA MUG OF COFFEE AT NIGHT.

1980

AND AT LAST, FROM 1980, THEY WERE ALLOWED TO BUY HEAVILY CENSORED NEWSPAPERS.

IN 1980 MK LAUNCHED A MILITARY CAMPAIGN, WHICH INCLUDED THE SABOTAGING OF STORAGE TANKS AT THE COUNTRY'S OIL REFINERY IN SECUNDA...

SUNDAY POST
'Free Mandela'

...EDITOR PERCY QOBOZA LAUNCHED A FREE MANDELA PETITION.

IT IS TIME FOR A PROGRAMME OF TOTAL ONSLAUGHT AGAINST COMMUNIST POWERS!

DEFENCE MINISTER MAGNUS MALAN TOOK A HARD LINE. ON ROBBEN ISLAND THE PRISONERS DISCUSSED HOW TO RESPOND.

MANDELA IMPRESSED THE YOUNGER MEN WITH HIS AUTHORITY AND HIS WILLINGNESS TO LISTEN.

6

THE NEGOTIATOR

THIS IS THE ENTRANCE TO THE VICTOR VERSTER PRISON FROM WHERE THE MOST FAMOUS PRISONER IN THE WORLD WAS RELEASED.

THERE WILL BE A PARLIAMENT WITH THREE HOUSES: ONE FOR WHITES, ONE FOR INDIANS AND ONE FOR COLOUREDS...THEY WILL BE ALLOWED TO VOTE ABOUT EDUCATION, HOUSING AND WELFARE...

HE IS AIMING TO LURE INDIANS AND COLOUREDS INTO BELIEVING HE IS MAKING REFORMS! BUT HE IS ISOLATING AFRICANS EVEN MORE...

MANDELA GREW A GARDEN IN THE COURTYARD. HE LIKED SPENDING TWO HOURS A DAY TENDING HIS PLANTS AND ON SUNDAYS SUPPLIED VEGETABLES FOR COMMON LAW PRISONERS.

TAMBO WAS RIGHT IN CALLING 1983 THE YEAR FOR UNITED ACTION! AND BOESAK HAS CALLED FOR A UNITED FRONT!

THE SOIL HAS BEEN PREPARED, NOW THEY CAN TAKE FORWARD THIS UNITED ACTION.

THE UNITED DEMOCRATIC FRONT (UDF) WAS LAUNCHED IN MITCHELLS PLAIN NEAR CAPE TOWN ON 20 AUGUST 1983.

FORWARD TO A NON-RACIAL AND DEMOCRATIC SOUTH AFRICA. FORWARD!

THE PRISONERS HEARD OF THE UDF LAUNCH FROM SISULU'S SON.

EQUAL RIGHTS FOR ALL

UDF SAYS NO TO NEW DEAL!

WE WANT FREEDOM

UDF

UDF UNITES

ALBERTINA SISULU CONTINUED TO SPEAK OUT. AT A 1994 UDF RALLY SHE SAID:

SONS AND DAUGHTERS OF AFRICA, TO ME TODAY I'M A GREAT BIG MOTHER, FOR TODAY OUR MULTIRACIAL BABY IS BORN, FOR TODAY OUR BABY THAT WILL RULE THIS SOUTH AFRICA IN FUTURE IS BORN, THE MULTIRACIAL BABY, THE UNITED DEMOCRATIC FRONT, WHICH IS UNITING PEOPLE TO SPEAK WITH ONE VOICE!

THE SAME DAY VIOLENCE ERUPTED AT SHARPEVILLE WHEN RESIDENTS MARCHED AGAINST RENT HIKES...

...THE UNREST SPREAD TO OTHER TOWNSHIPS LEAVING 30 PEOPLE DEAD AND OVER 300 INJURED.

THE ARMY OCCUPIED TOWNSHIPS, STUDENTS BOYCOTTED SCHOOL AND WORKERS STAYED AT HOME...

UNBELIEVABLE THAT BOTHA CAN SAY IT IS NOT THE GOVERNMENT STANDING IN THE WAY OF YOUR FREEDOM. BUT THAT IT IS YOU!

WE ONLY TURNED TO ARMED STRUGGLE AFTER THEY CLOSED THE DOOR TO PEACEFUL PROTEST. IT IS BOTHA WHO SHOULD RENOUNCE VIOLENCE!

BECAUSE YOU WILL NOT RENOUNCE THE ARMED STRUGGLE!

HE HAS MADE A PUBLIC CHALLENGE AND I WILL MAKE A PUBLIC RESPONSE.

MANDELA, SISULU, KATHRADA, MLANGENI AND MHLABA ALL REJECTED THE OFFER IN A LETTER TO PRESIDENT BOTHA.

MANDELA PREPARED A STATEMENT TO BE READ BY ZINDZI AT A RALLY AT SOWETO'S JABULANI STADIUM ON 10 FEBRUARY. HE GAVE IT TO WINNIE DURING A VISIT.

YOU MUST STOP TALKING ABOUT POLITICS!

THIS IS A MATTER OF NATIONAL IMPORTANCE! IF YOU WANT ME TO STOP, YOU'D BETTER GET DIRECT ORDERS FROM THE PRESIDENT...

My father says...
What freedom am I being offered while the organisation of the people remains banned?
What freedom am I being offered when I may be arrested on a pass offence?
What freedom am I being offered to live my life as a family with my dear wife who remains in banishment in Brandfort?
What freedom am I being offered when I must ask for permission to live in an urban area... when my very South African citizenship is not respected?
Only free men can negotiate. Prisoners cannot enter into contracts...
I cannot and will not give any undertaking at a time when I and you, the people, are not free. Your freedom and mine cannot be separated.

I will return!

IT WAS A POWERFUL MESSAGE. THE PEOPLE WERE MOVED...

BOTHA WAS IN TROUBLE...

WE HAVE PAINTED OURSELVES INTO A CORNER... A TOTAL DEADLOCK!

ABOUT 20 RADIO NEWS BULLETINS A DAY KEPT THE PRISONERS UP-TO-DATE WITH WORLD EVENTS...

...TODAY ON THE 25TH ANNIVERSARY OF SHARPEVILLE 19 PEOPLE DIED IN UITENHAGE DURING A CLASH BETWEEN THE POLICE AND PROTESTORS...

AMANDLA!

...WINNIE MANDELA WAS ON THE FRONTLINE OF THE STRUGGLE AND HAD BECOME A LEADER IN HER OWN RIGHT...

...THE UDF WAS BLAMED FOR THE UNREST, THOUSANDS WERE DETAINED, TORTURED AND ABDUCTED.

WE BID FAREWELL TO THESE COMRADES...

REV. BEYERS NAUDE SPOKE AT THE FUNERAL OF THE CRADOCK FOUR WHO HAD BEEN ABDUCTED AND MURDERED BY THE SECURITY POLICE.

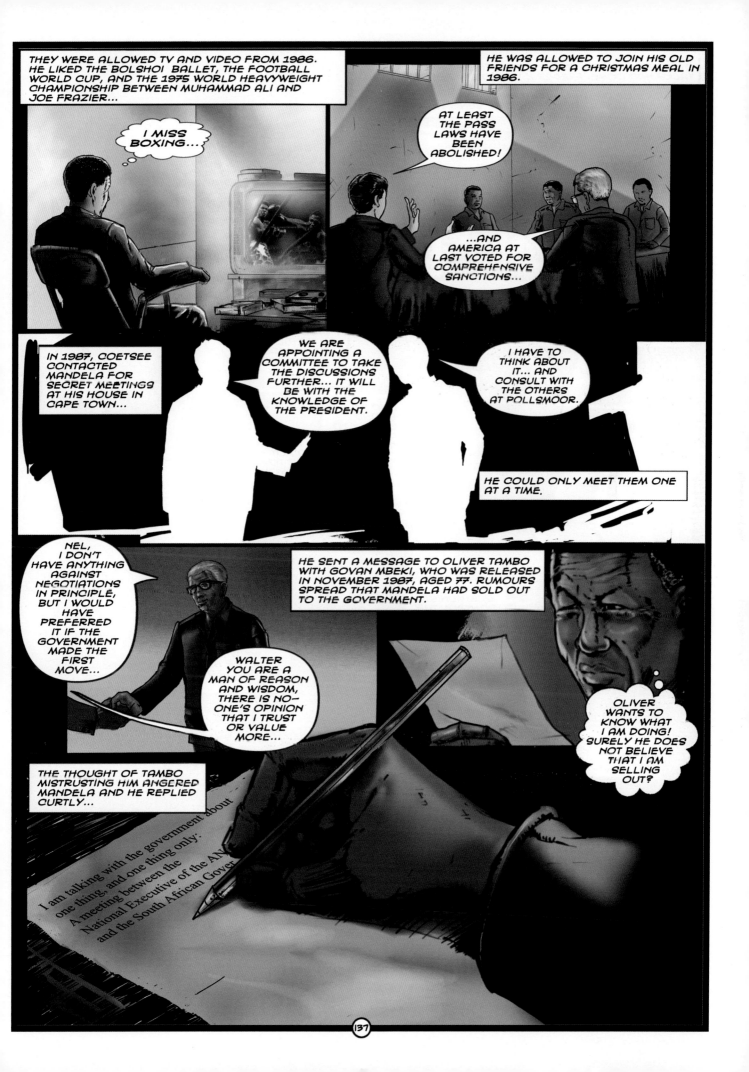

THEY WERE ALLOWED TV AND VIDEO FROM 1986. HE LIKED THE BOLSHOI BALLET, THE FOOTBALL WORLD CUP, AND THE 1975 WORLD HEAVYWEIGHT CHAMPIONSHIP BETWEEN MUHAMMAD ALI AND JOE FRAZIER...

I MISS BOXING...

HE WAS ALLOWED TO JOIN HIS OLD FRIENDS FOR A CHRISTMAS MEAL IN 1986.

AT LEAST THE PASS LAWS HAVE BEEN ABOLISHED!

...AND AMERICA AT LAST VOTED FOR COMPREHENSIVE SANCTIONS...

IN 1987, COETSEE CONTACTED MANDELA FOR SECRET MEETINGS AT HIS HOUSE IN CAPE TOWN...

WE ARE APPOINTING A COMMITTEE TO TAKE THE DISCUSSIONS FURTHER... IT WILL BE WITH THE KNOWLEDGE OF THE PRESIDENT.

I HAVE TO THINK ABOUT IT... AND CONSULT WITH THE OTHERS AT POLLSMOOR.

HE COULD ONLY MEET THEM ONE AT A TIME.

NEL, I DON'T HAVE ANYTHING AGAINST NEGOTIATIONS IN PRINCIPLE, BUT I WOULD HAVE PREFERRED IT IF THE GOVERNMENT MADE THE FIRST MOVE...

WALTER YOU ARE A MAN OF REASON AND WISDOM, THERE IS NO-ONE'S OPINION THAT I TRUST OR VALUE MORE...

HE SENT A MESSAGE TO OLIVER TAMBO WITH GOVAN MBEKI, WHO WAS RELEASED IN NOVEMBER 1987, AGED 77. RUMOURS SPREAD THAT MANDELA HAD SOLD OUT TO THE GOVERNMENT.

OLIVER WANTS TO KNOW WHAT I AM DOING! SURELY HE DOES NOT BELIEVE THAT I AM SELLING OUT?

THE THOUGHT OF TAMBO MISTRUSTING HIM ANGERED MANDELA AND HE REPLIED CURTLY...

I am talking with the government about one thing, and one thing only. A meeting between the National Executive of the ANC and the South African Gover

OTHERS ALSO REALISED THAT THE TIME FOR TALKS HAD COME. FREDERIK VAN ZYL SLABBERT, FORMER OPPOSITION LEADER, ARRANGED FOR MEMBERS OF THE ANC AND AFRIKANER INTELLECTUALS TO MEET IN DAKAR, SENEGAL.

I HAVE NO IDEA HOW THIS WILL TURN OUT... BUT I HAVE TO PUSH FORWARD.

EVEN AS MANDELA WAS PREPARING TO MEET WITH THE GOVERNMENT TEAM, THE UDF AND 17 OTHER ORGANISATIONS WERE BANNED.

IN MAY 1988 HE MET WITH COETSEE, TWO PRISON OFFICIALS AND NIËL BARNARD, THE HEAD OF THE NATIONAL INTELLIGENCE SERVICE.

PRESIDENT BOTHA WILL NOT MEET WITH YOU UNTIL YOU RENOUNCE ALL VIOLENCE.

THE ANC WILL RESPOND PEACEFULLY TO PEACEFUL METHODS...

WE DO NOT WANT TO DRIVE YOU INTO THE SEA!

...SOUTH AFRICA BELONGS TO ALL WHO LIVE IN IT, BLACK AND WHITE.

BUT COMMUNISTS CONTROL THE ANC!

COMMUNISTS IN THE ANC ARE FAR FROM BEING AN EVIL EMPIRE! WE WILL NEVER BE CONTROLLED BY ANYONE.

72 000 PEOPLE WATCHED A 'FREEDOM AT 70' CONCERT FOR MANDELA AT WEMBLEY STADIUM IN LONDON AND 200 MILLION SAW IT ON TV.

MANDELA WAS SHOCKED WHEN HIS HOME IN SOWETO WAS TORCHED BY ANGRY YOUTHS.

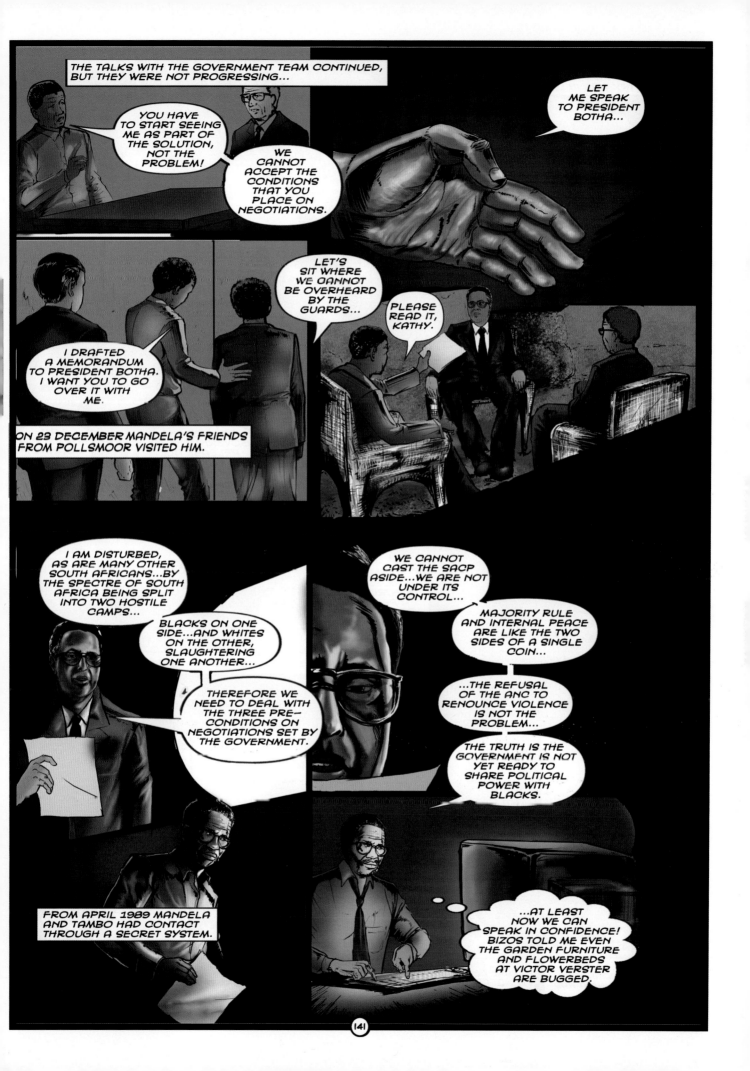

A WEEK LATER... AFTER WORKING THROUGH THE NIGHT ON A SPEECH WITH COLLEAGUES, MANDELA PREPARED FOR HIS RELEASE...

AS HE TOOK HIS FIRST STEPS TO FREEDOM MANDELA WAS GREETED BY JOURNALISTS FROM ALL OVER THE WORLD, AND THOUSANDS OF SUPPORTERS. THEY DANCED, CHEERED AND CRIED WITH HAPPINESS. THEIR CHANCE FOR A NEW FUTURE HAD COME...

7
PRESIDENT-IN-WAITING

THIS IS GROOTE SCHUUR, WHERE THE FIRST BREAKTHROUGH IN NEGOTIATIONS BETWEEN THE ANC AND THE APARTHEID GOVERNMENT TOOK PLACE...

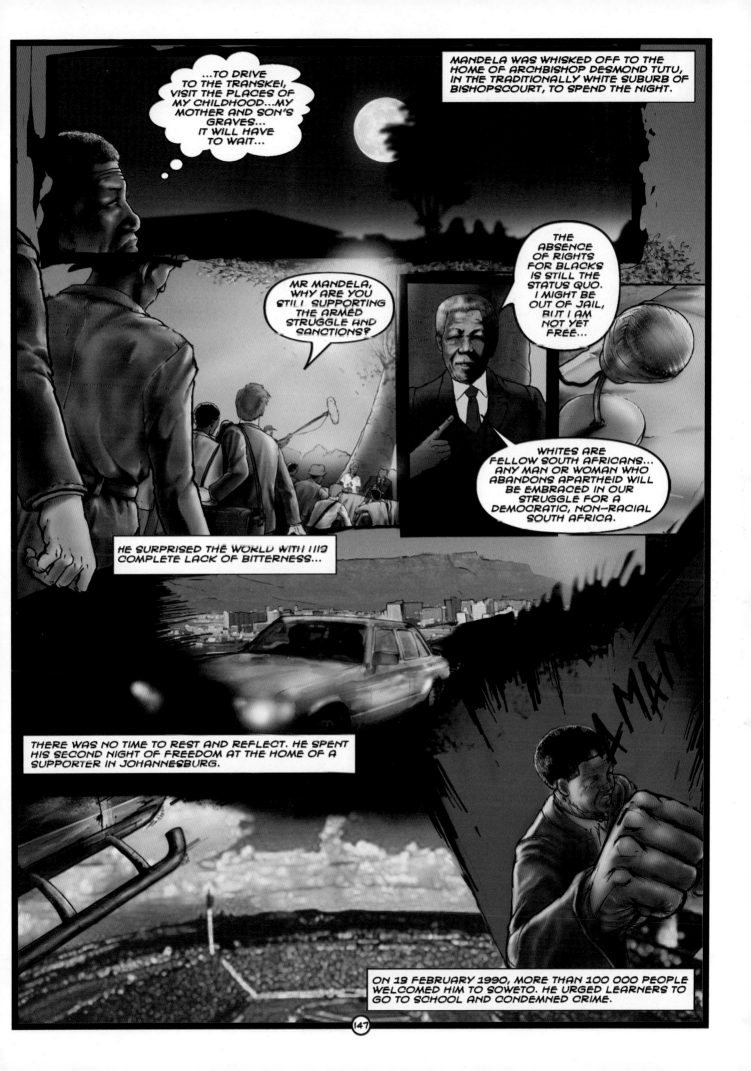

MANDELA VISITED AFRICAN COUNTRIES, EUROPE, AND NORTH AMERICA. HE RECEIVED A HERO'S WELCOME WHEREVER HE WENT. IN NEW YORK A TICKER TAPE PARADE WAS HELD IN HIS HONOUR.

THE EMPIRE STATE BUILDING WAS LIT UP IN THE ANC COLOURS.

HE STAYED AT GRACIE MANSION. A FAR CRY FROM THE DAMP CELL HE HAD BECOME USED TO.

JUST A QUICK JOG AND I WILL BE READY FOR THE DAY...

BUT HE SOON REALISED THAT EVEN HERE HIS FREEDOM WAS NOT COMPLETE...

STOP! IT IS TOO DANGEROUS. WE HAVE TO SEND A GUARD WITH YOU.

HE MET WITH MARGARET THATCHER, THE BRITISH PRIME MINISTER WHO HAD OPPOSED SANCTIONS AGAINST SOUTH AFRICA.

HOW CAN YOU TALK TO SOMEONE WHO HAS DENOUNCED YOU AS A TERRORIST?

I AM WORKING WITH SOUTH AFRICANS WHO HAVE DONE MUCH WORSE THINGS...

SHE EVEN WARNED ME TO TAKE BETTER CARE OF MYSELF!

WHEN MANDELA RETURNED TO SOUTH AFRICA IN JULY VIOLENCE AROUND JOHANNESBURG HAD INCREASED DRAMATICALLY. HUNDREDS OF PEOPLE WERE KILLED.

THEY ARE PLANNING SOMETHING! WE HAVE NOTIFIED THE MINISTER OF LAW AND ORDER...WE HAVE ASKED HIM TO PROTECT THE PEOPLE!

MR. DE KLERK, 30 PEOPLE WERE KILLED, HUNDREDS WERE INJURED! YOU WERE WARNED IN ADVANCE... AND YET YOU DID NOTHING! WHY IS THAT? WHY HAVE THE POLICE SAT ON THEIR HANDS?

ON 22 JULY, MEN ARMED WITH TRADITIONAL WEAPONS WERE BUSSED TO SEBOKENG, WHERE THEY ATTACKED FAMILIES AS THEY SLEPT.

JUST AS MANDELA CONFRONTED DE KLERK ABOUT VIOLENCE, DE KLERK LATER CONFRONTED MANDELA ABOUT OPERATION VULA.

153

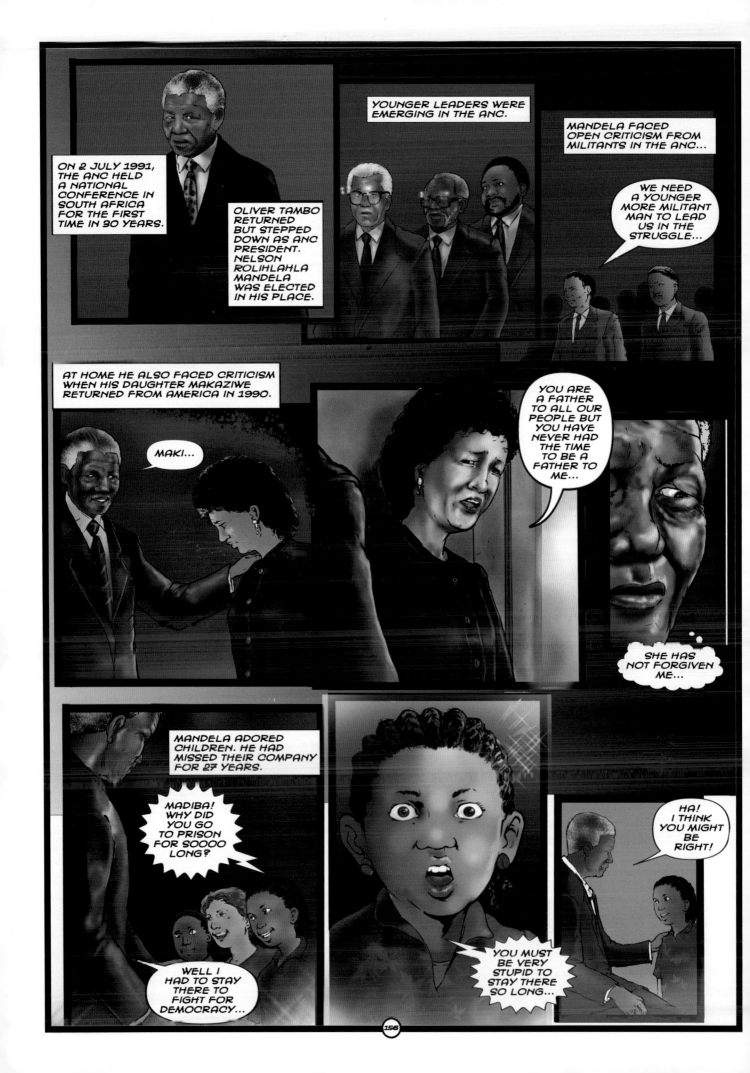

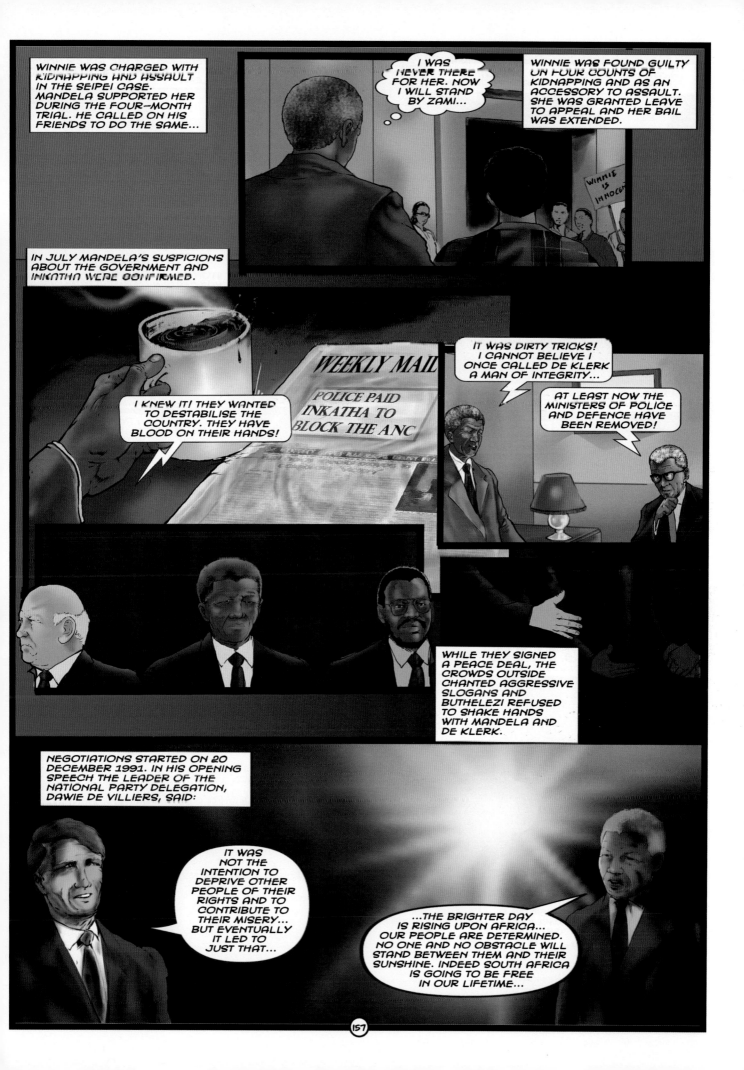

INKATHA AND RIGHT–WING AFRIKANER PARTIES DID NOT PARTICIPATE IN CODESA.

...THE ANC IS HIDING ARMS! IT IS KEEPING MK AS A PRIVATE ARMY...

SO THAT IS WHY HE WANTED TO BE THE LAST SPEAKER! HE IS ADMONISHING US LIKE WE ARE SCHOOL CHILDREN!

MANDELA BROKE THE RULES AND LAUNCHED A COUNTER–ATTACK ON DE KLERK.

EVEN THE HEAD OF AN ILLEGITIMATE, DISCREDITED MINORITY REGIME, SUCH AS HIS, HAS CERTAIN STANDARDS TO UPHOLD!

MIRACULOUSLY NEGOTIATIONS DID NOT BREAK DOWN AGAIN.

BUT IN HIS PERSONAL LIFE MANDELA WAS EXPERIENCING BREAKDOWN. AT A PRESS CONFERENCE ON 19 APRIL 1992 HE ANNOUNCED THE END OF HIS MARRIAGE TO WINNIE.

I PART WITH MY WIFE WITH NO RECRIMINATIONS... I HOPE YOU APPRECIATE THE PAIN I HAVE GONE THROUGH.

MANDELA'S SADNESS WAS VISIBLE. IN HIS SPEECH AT ZINDZI'S WEDDING HE SAID...

TO BE THE FATHER OF A NATION IS A GREAT HONOUR, BUT TO BE THE FATHER OF A FAMILY IS A GREATER JOY...

BUT IT WAS A JOY I HAD FAR TOO LITTLE OF...

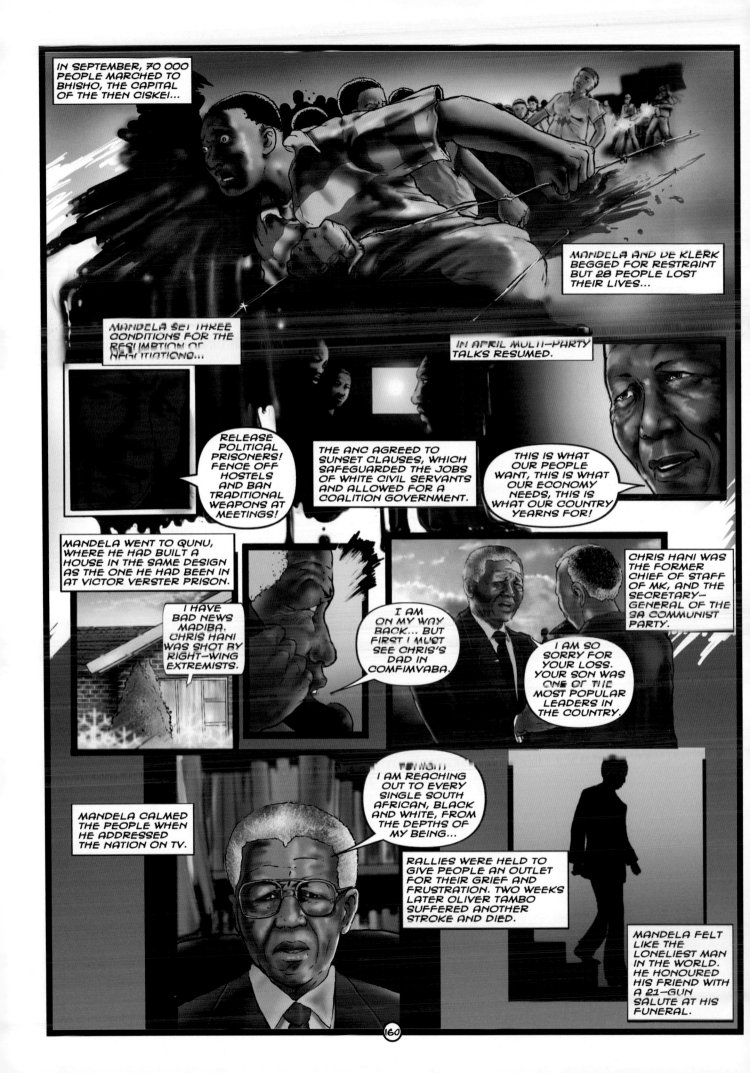

ON 2 JUNE 1993, THE APPEAL COURT UPHELD WINNIE'S CONVICTION FOR KIDNAPPING IN THE STOMPIE SEIPEI CASE, BUT RULED SHE HAD NOT BEEN AN ACCESSORY TO ASSAULT. SHE RECEIVED A ONE-YEAR SUSPENDED SENTENCE AND WAS FINED R15 000.

AMANDLA!!!

THE COUNTDOWN TO THE DEMOCRATIC TRANSFER OF POWER TO THE PEOPLE HAS BEGUN.

THE SAME DAY MANDELA TASTED VICTORY WHEN AGREEMENT WAS REACHED ON AN ELECTION DATE.

FIRST DEMOCRATIC ELECTIONS DATE 27 APRIL 1994

ON 25 JUNE 1993, HUNDREDS OF THUGS FROM THE AWB, A SMALL RIGHT-WING MILITANT GROUP, DESCENDED ON THE WORLD TRADE CENTRE.

THEY CRASHED THROUGH THE GLASS DOORS, URINATED ON CARPETS AND HELD A BARBEQUE.

THE AZANIAN PEOPLE'S LIBERATION ARMY (APLA), ATTACKED WORSHIPPERS AT ST. JAMES' CHURCH, IN CAPE TOWN, KILLING 11 PEOPLE AND INJURING 55 MORE.

THE ANC'S AND NP'S CHIEF NEGOTIATORS, RAMAPHOSA AND MEYER, SOMETIMES STRUGGLED TO CONVINCE THEIR PARTIES TO ACCEPT THEIR PROPOSALS. A BIG BREAKTHROUGH CAME ON 18 NOVEMBER WHEN AN INTERIM CONSTITUION WAS AGREED TO.

I WILL NOT BUDGE! MAJORITY RULE WILL APPLY.

MINORITIES MUST BE SAFE-GUARDED!

WE DID IT! THEY ACCEPTED OUR COMPROMISE BETWEEN POWER-SHARING AND MAJORITY RULE!

YES! IT WAS TOUGH CONVINCING THEM BUT THE NP NOW AGREES TO MAJORITY RULE...

AS SOON AS THE DEAL WAS STRUCK THE CELEBRATIONS STARTED.

NOT EVERYONE WAS HAPPY. INKATHA AND THE CONSERVATIVE PARTY DID NOT RECOGNISE THE AGREEMENT, AND MANY AFRIKANERS FELT DE KLERK SOLD THEM OUT.

IN DECEMBER, MANDELA AND DE KLERK JOINTLY RECEIVED THE NOBEL PEACE PRIZE.

AT THE NOBEL CEREMONY IN OSLO, MANDELA SAID:

...LET IT NEVER BE SAID BY FUTURE GENERATIONS THAT INDIFFERENCE, CYNICISM OR SELFISHNESS...

...MADE US FAIL TO LIVE UP TO THE IDEALS OF HUMANISM, WHICH THE NOBEL PEACE PRIZE ENCAPSULATES...

162

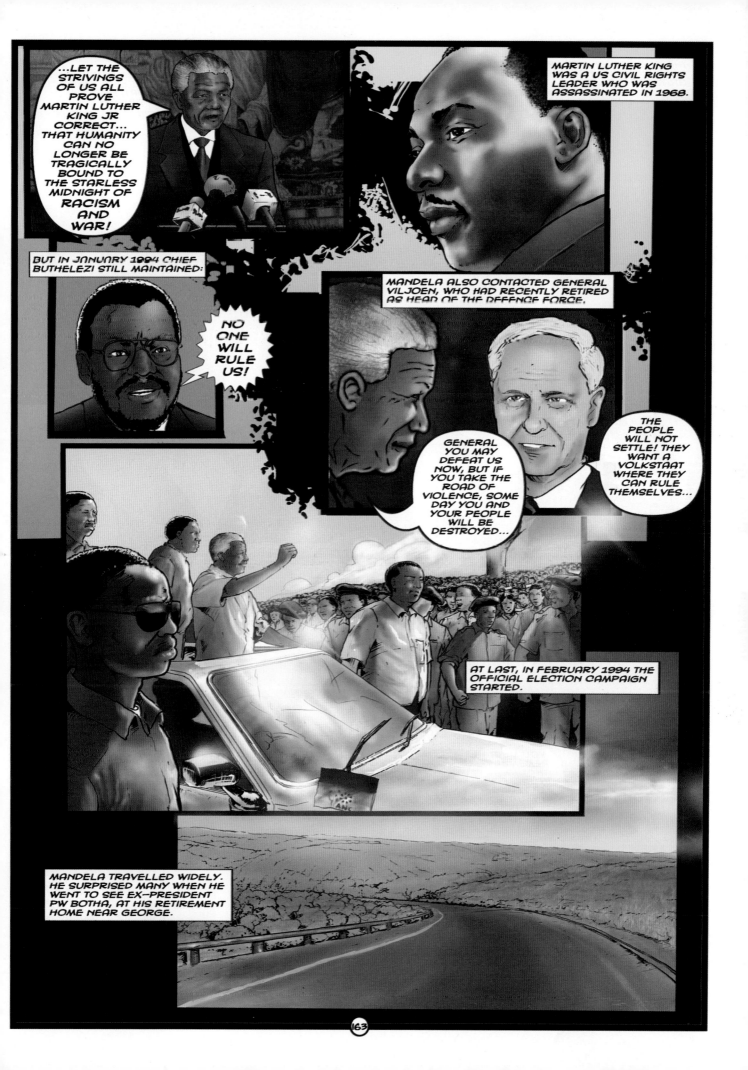

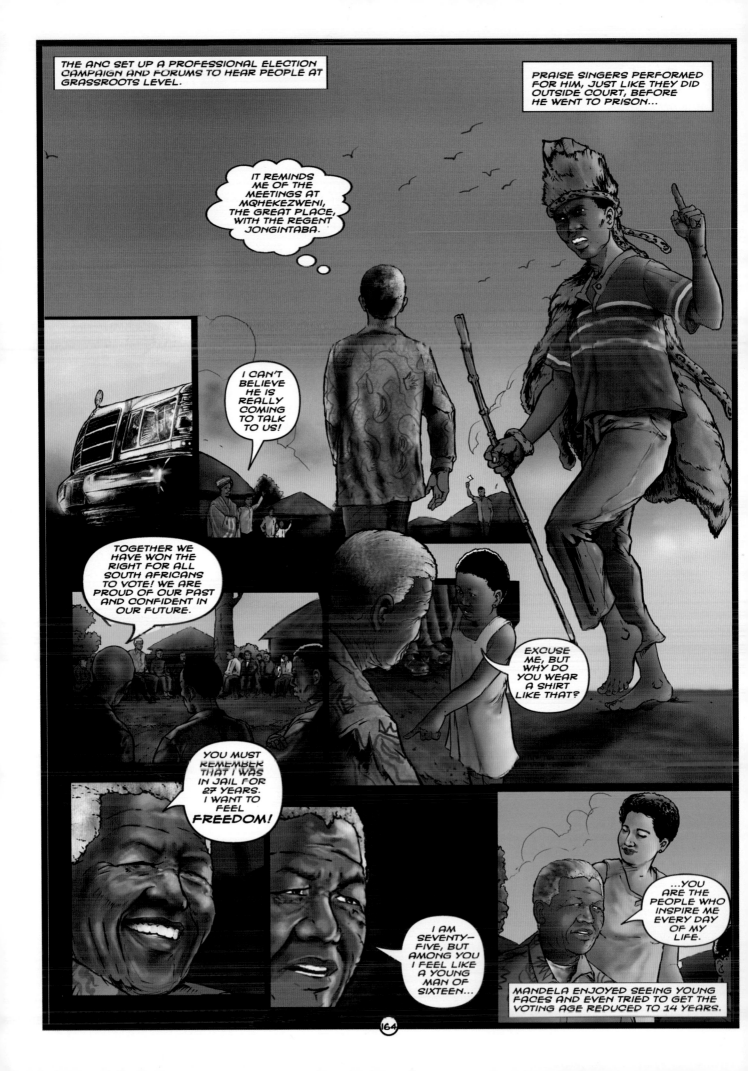

THE ANC SET UP A PROFESSIONAL ELECTION CAMPAIGN AND FORUMS TO HEAR PEOPLE AT GRASSROOTS LEVEL.

PRAISE SINGERS PERFORMED FOR HIM, JUST LIKE THEY DID OUTSIDE COURT, BEFORE HE WENT TO PRISON...

IT REMINDS ME OF THE MEETINGS AT MQHEKEZWENI, THE GREAT PLACE, WITH THE REGENT JONGINTABA.

I CAN'T BELIEVE HE IS REALLY COMING TO TALK TO US!

TOGETHER WE HAVE WON THE RIGHT FOR ALL SOUTH AFRICANS TO VOTE! WE ARE PROUD OF OUR PAST AND CONFIDENT IN OUR FUTURE.

EXCUSE ME, BUT WHY DO YOU WEAR A SHIRT LIKE THAT?

YOU MUST REMEMBER THAT I WAS IN JAIL FOR 27 YEARS. I WANT TO FEEL FREEDOM!

I AM SEVENTY-FIVE, BUT AMONG YOU I FEEL LIKE A YOUNG MAN OF SIXTEEN...

...YOU ARE THE PEOPLE WHO INSPIRE ME EVERY DAY OF MY LIFE.

MANDELA ENJOYED SEEING YOUNG FACES AND EVEN TRIED TO GET THE VOTING AGE REDUCED TO 14 YEARS.

FROM BEFORE SUNRISE ON 27 APRIL 1994 PEOPLE FLOCKED TO VOTE MOST, FOR THE FIRST TIME IN THIER LIVES.

MANDELA VOTED AT OHLANGE HIGH SCHOOL IN KWAZULU-NATAL NEAR THE GRAVE OF JOHN DUBE, THE FIRST PRESIDENT OF THE ANC.

MR MANDELA! WHO ARE YOU VOTING FOR?

I HAVE BEEN TRYING TO MAKE A DECISION ALL MORNING!

THE ELECTION WAS CLOSELY WATCHED BY THE WORLD. ABOUT 200,000 OBSERVERS AND OFFICIALS WITNESSED 29 MILLION PEOPLE VOTING PEACEFULLY.

AT LAST IT WAS ANNOUNCED THAT THE ANC WON 62,6 PERCENT OF THE VOTES. MANDELA WAS PLEASED THAT IT WAS NOT A TWO-THIRDS MAJORITY WHICH WOULD HAVE ALLOWED THE ANC TO CHANGE THE CONSTITUTION.

THE PEOPLE OF SOUTH AFRICA HAD SPOKEN. ON 2 MAY DE KLERK MADE A CONCESSION SPEECH IN PRETORIA AND PRAISED MANDELA AS A MAN OF DESTINY.

THE ANC HELD AN ELECTION VICTORY PARTY IN JOHANNESBURG. MANDELA WAS EXHAUSTED BUT CELEBRATED WITH HIS COMRADES.

FREE AT LAST! FREE AT LAST!

I STAND BEFORE YOU HUMBLED BY YOUR COURAGE, WITH A HEART FULL OF LOVE FOR ALL OF YOU...

THIS IS THE TIME TO HEAL OLD WOUNDS AND BUILD A NEW SOUTH AFRICA!

THE WORLD SAW MANDELA CELEBRATING WITH A DANCE THAT WAS SOON TO BECOME HIS TRADEMARK. BUT WHAT DID THE FUTURE HOLD FOR THE FLEDGLING DEMOCRACY AT THE TIP OF AFRICA?

8
MR PRESIDENT

WE'RE OUTSIDE THE HOUSES OF PARLIAMENT IN CAPE TOWN, WHERE NELSON MANDELA WAS NOMINATED AS PRESIDENT OF SOUTH AFRICA AND WAS UNANIMOUSLY ELECTED BY MEMBERS OF PARLIAMENT.

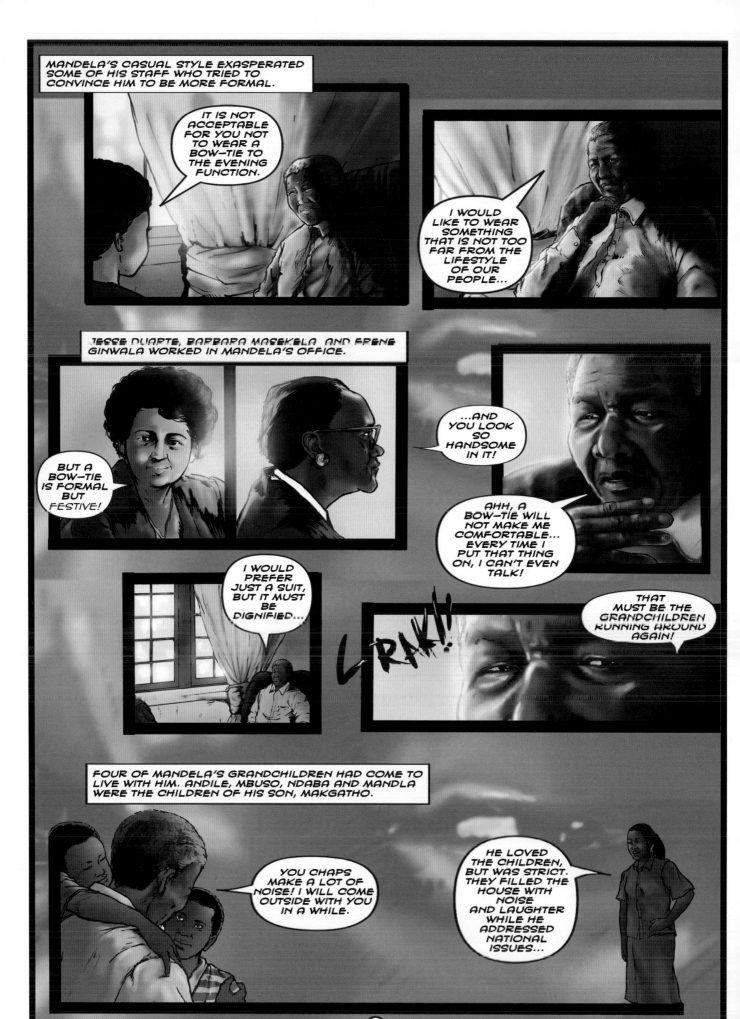

ON THE FIFTH ANNIVERSARY OF HIS RELEASE FROM PRISON HE RETURNED TO ROBBEN ISLAND FOR A REUNION OF FORMER POLITICAL PRISONERS.

MOTHER... THEMBI... SO MANY PEOPLE WERE LOST TO ME WHILE I WAS HERE...

A FEW DAYS LATER THE 'OLD MAN', AS MANY YOUNGER MP'S REFERRED TO HIM, OPENED PARLIAMENT IN THE SAME RELAXED ATMOSPHERE HE CREATED IN 1994.

MANY NEW MP'S STILL COULD NOT BELIEVE THAT THESE FORMER 'TERRORISTS' WERE NOW LAWMAKERS.

FROM PRISON TO PARLIAMENT!

MANDELA'S SCHEDULE WAS RELENTLESS. HIS STAFF AND SECURITY GUARDS HAD THEIR HANDS FULL.

STOP THE CAR! I NEED TO GO TO THOSE STREET CHILDREN.
TATA, IT IS TOO DANGEROUS!
MANDELA LOVED CHILDREN AND COULD NOT STAND SEEING THEM SUFFER...
IT IS YOUR JOB TO PROTECT ME!
IT'S NELSON MANDELA!
MADIBA! IT IS YOU!
WHY DO YOU LOVE US?
WHY DO YOU ASK THAT?
BECAUSE YOU ALWAYS TRY TO HELP US!
OHH... I TRY TO HELP BUT IT IS NEVER ENOUGH...
LATER THAT NIGHT...
I WILL SET UP A CHILDREN'S FUND...
IT IS POSSIBLE FOR ME TO DONATE A THIRD OF MY SALARY EVERY MONTH...
THERE ARE CHILDREN IN NEED EVERYWHERE!

CELEBRITIES, BUSINESS MOGULS, ROCK STARS AND POLITICIANS FLOCKED TO SEE HIM, BUT HE INSISTED ON SPENDING CHRISTMAS WITH HIS FAMILY IN THE TRANSKEI.

ON CHRISTMAS DAY HE WENT FOR HIS USUAL EARLY MORNING WALK ON THE PATHS IN AND AROUND THE VILLAGES OF HIS CHILDHOOD.

WALKING HERE IS A LINK TO THE PAST THAT I HAVE MISSED... THE VILLAGERS HAVE SUCH CONFIDENCE IN US...IT IS A GREAT RESPONSIBILITY...

HE THOUGHT BACK TO CHRISTMASSES PAST AND STOPPED TO TALK TO EVERYONE HE SAW.

HE GREETED EVERYONE AND ASKED EACH CHILD THEIR NAME, AGE AND WHERE THEY WENT TO SCHOOL.

THAT IS VERY GOOD! MY NAME IS MANDELA.

I AM VUKILE, I AM SEVEN, AND I AM IN GRADE THREE.

HE AGREED TO HAVE SOME JOURNALISTS JOIN HIM ON HIS WALK. SOME STRUGGLED TO KEEP UP WITH THE FIT 77-YEAR-OLD WHO WALKED FOR THREE HOURS.

WHEN I WAS A BOY HERDING CATTLE OR SHEEP MY DUTIES WOULD END EARLIER THAN USUAL ON CHRISTMAS.

ON THIS DAY WE CAME HOME FOR THE ONLY CUP OF TEA OF THE YEAR...

THEY GAVE US FOOD... WHAT ELDERLY PEOPLE DO, THEY EAT AND THEY KEEP ON GIVING YOU A PIECE. SOMETIMES IT IS ENOUGH TO FEED YOU...

FAMILY HELPED HIM HAND OUT CHUNKS OF MEAT TO WAITING CHILDREN. HE MADE SURE THEY WERE FED BEFORE THE ADULTS.

MANDELA HOSTED A CHRISTMAS PARTY FOR CHILDREN EVERY YEAR. HE STARTED THE TRADITION IN QUNU, FOR THE POOR CHILDREN IN THE AREA.

SOME OF THESE CHILDREN HAVE BEEN WALKING FOR HOURS TO BE HERE...

IT IS A FORLORN ATTEMPT. THEY GO BACK TO THEIR SQUALOR, THEIR MISERY...

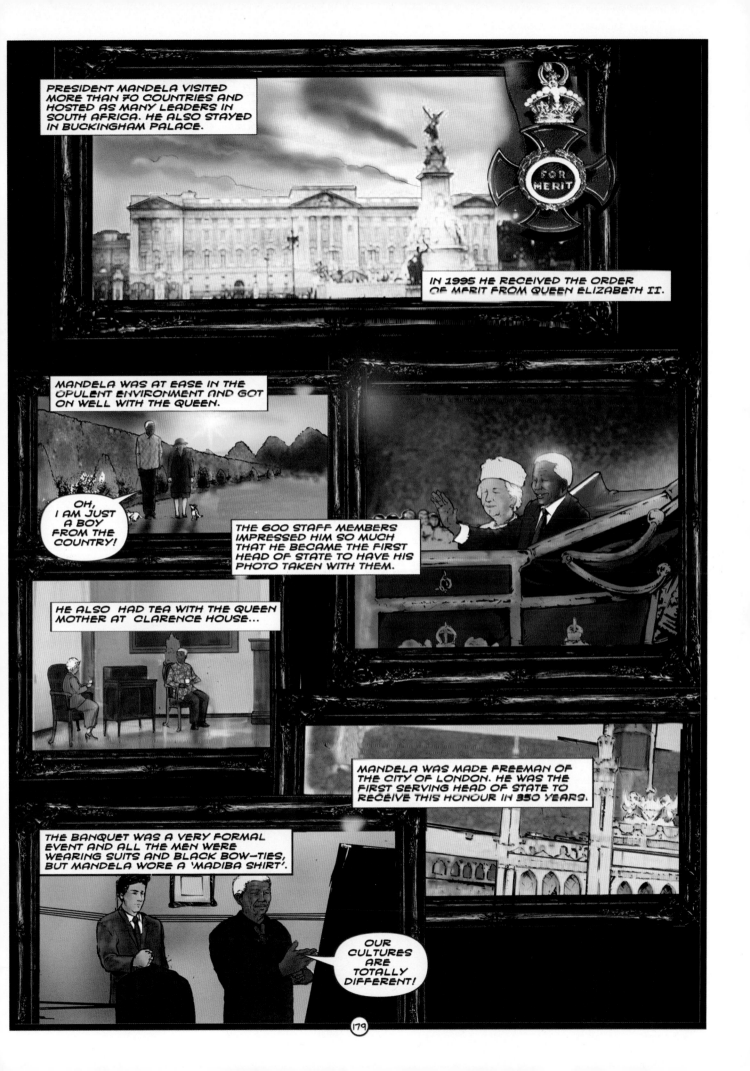

PRESIDENT MANDELA VISITED MORE THAN 70 COUNTRIES AND HOSTED AS MANY LEADERS IN SOUTH AFRICA. HE ALSO STAYED IN BUCKINGHAM PALACE.

FOR MERIT

IN 1995 HE RECEIVED THE ORDER OF MERIT FROM QUEEN ELIZABETH II.

MANDELA WAS AT EASE IN THE OPULENT ENVIRONMENT AND GOT ON WELL WITH THE QUEEN.

OH, I AM JUST A BOY FROM THE COUNTRY!

THE 600 STAFF MEMBERS IMPRESSED HIM SO MUCH THAT HE BECAME THE FIRST HEAD OF STATE TO HAVE HIS PHOTO TAKEN WITH THEM.

HE ALSO HAD TEA WITH THE QUEEN MOTHER AT CLARENCE HOUSE...

MANDELA WAS MADE FREEMAN OF THE CITY OF LONDON. HE WAS THE FIRST SERVING HEAD OF STATE TO RECEIVE THIS HONOUR IN 350 YEARS.

THE BANQUET WAS A VERY FORMAL EVENT AND ALL THE MEN WERE WEARING SUITS AND BLACK BOW-TIES, BUT MANDELA WORE A 'MADIBA SHIRT'.

OUR CULTURES ARE TOTALLY DIFFERENT!

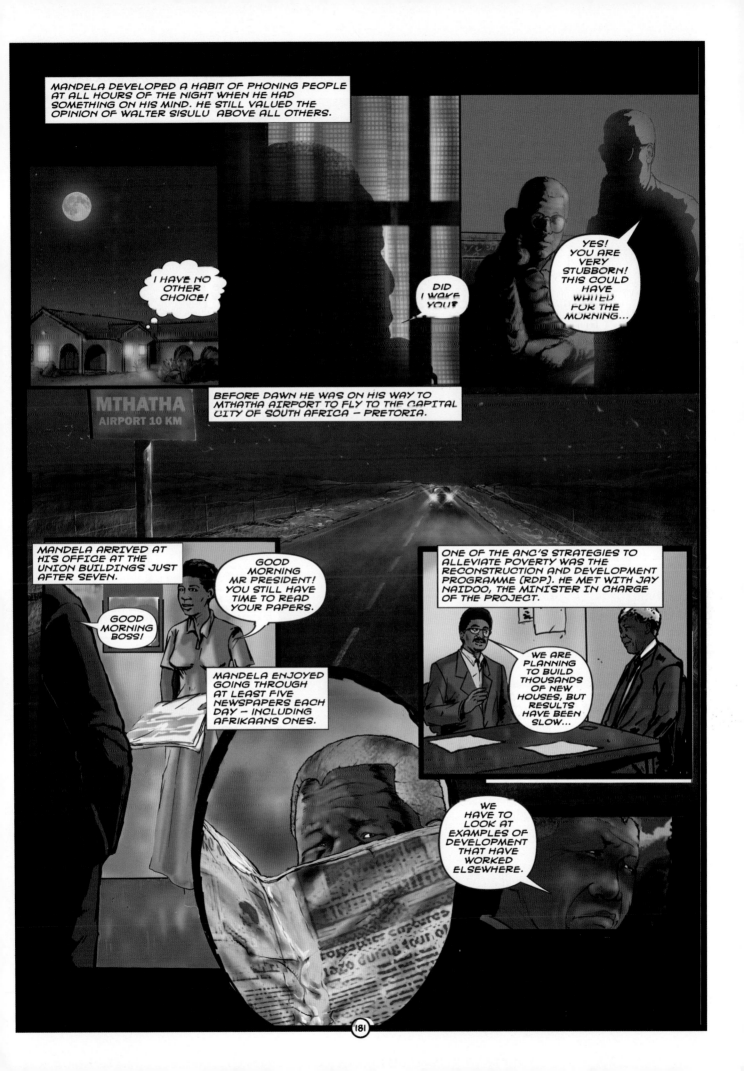

AFTER A FULL DAY OF MEETINGS, INCLUDING THE SWEARING-IN OF A NEW DEPUTY MINISTER TO REPLACE HIS ESTRANGED WIFE, MANDELA BOARDED A PLANE TO CAPE TOWN.

AT NEETHLINGSHOF WINE FARM HE ADDRESSED A MOSTLY WHITE AUDIENCE OF BUSINESS LEADERS ABOUT ECONOMIC RECONSTRUCTION.

MY WARDER AT VICTOR VERSTER TOLD ME THE BEST WINES WERE DRY. BUT I ALWAYS THOUGHT ALL WINE WAS WET!

IN 1995 HE CHANGED THE NAME OF LIBERTAS TO MAHLAMBA NDLOPFU. IT COMES FROM A SHANGAAN EXPRESSION MEANING "NEW DAWN".

ALTHOUGH MANDELA MADE MANY NEW RICH AND FAMOUS FRIENDS, HE KEPT CLOSE TO HIS OLD COMRADES LIKE AHMED KATHRADA.

AHHH! LUNCH IS HERE! AND ON TIME!

OH MADIBA IT IS SAMP AND BEANS! JAIL FOOD IS STILL YOUR FAVOURITE!

YES! DO YOU REMEMBER HOW AFRICANS WERE NOT ALLOWED TO HAVE BREAD FOR SIXTEEN YEARS?

MANDELA WAS A SYMBOL FOR AFRICAN DEMOCRACY AND BECAME INVOLVED IN INTERNATIONAL ISSUES.

AT HIS FIRST COMMONWEALTH SUMMIT IN 1995, HE ASKED FOR THE RELEASE FROM PRISON OF HUMAN RIGHTS ACTIVISTS IN NIGERIA.

ABACHA HAD ARRESTED KEN SARO-WIWA AND HIS COLLEAGUES AND CONDEMNED THEM TO DEATH.

MANDELA WAS DEEPLY DISAPPOINTED WHEN ABACHA HAD SARO-WIWA AND EIGHT OTHER ACTIVISTS EXECUTED.

HE WAS REGULARLY CALLED TO HELP END VARIOUS INTERNATIONAL CRISES. IN DECEMBER 1999 HE WAS APPOINTED AS MEDIATOR IN THE BURUNDI PEACE TALKS BASED IN TANZANIA.

MANDELA ALSO TRAVELLED TO INDONESIA WHERE HE PERSUADED THE DICTATOR, SUHARTO, TO LET HIM SEE XANANA GUSMAO, THE JAILED HERO OF EAST TIMOR'S STRUGGLE.

MR GUSMAO MUST BE RELEASED FROM PRISON TO BE ABLE TO NEGOTIATE...

GUSMAO WAS RELEASED IN 1998 AND WAS LATER ELECTED PRESIDENT OF EAST TIMOR, WHICH RECEIVED ITS INDEPENDENCE FROM INDONESIA.

IN 1998 SOUTH AFRICA HOSTED THE 12TH SUMMIT OF THE NON-ALIGNED MOVEMENT IN DURBAN.

IN MAY 1996 DE KLERK LEFT THE GOVERNMENT OF NATIONAL UNITY AND PLEDGED A VIGOROUS OPPOSITION BUT SOON RETIRED FROM POLITICS.

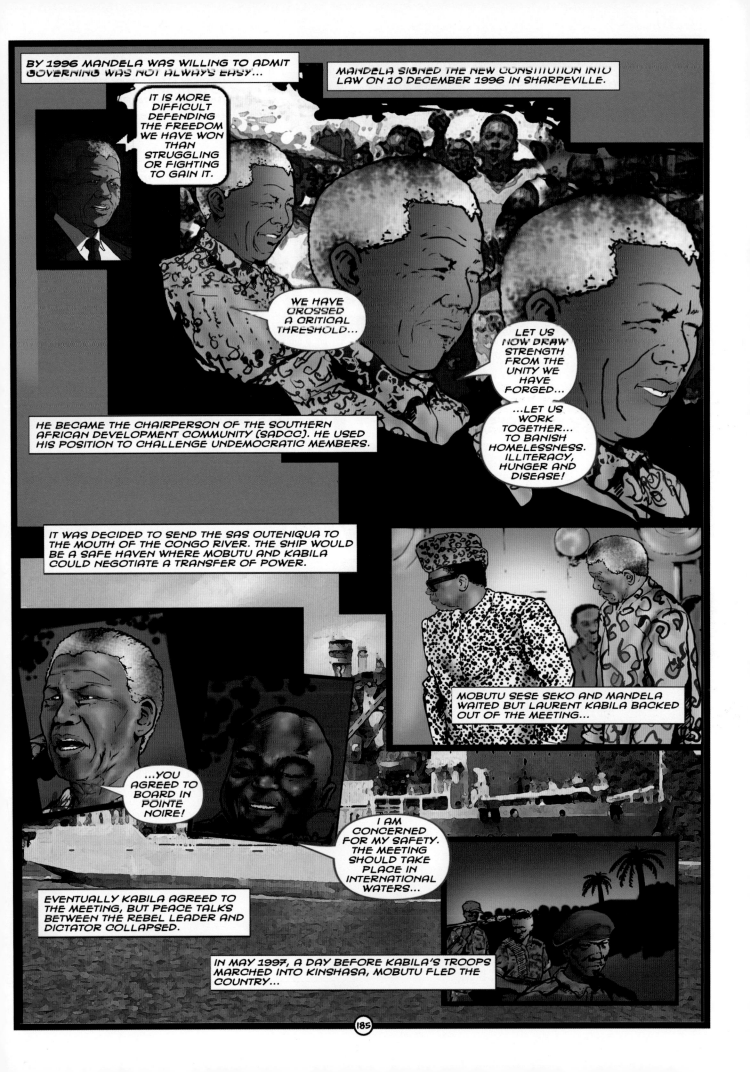

BY 1996 MANDELA WAS WILLING TO ADMIT GOVERNING WAS NOT ALWAYS EASY...

IT IS MORE DIFFICULT DEFENDING THE FREEDOM WE HAVE WON THAN STRUGGLING OR FIGHTING TO GAIN IT.

WE HAVE CROSSED A CRITICAL THRESHOLD...

MANDELA SIGNED THE NEW CONSTITUTION INTO LAW ON 10 DECEMBER 1996 IN SHARPEVILLE.

LET US NOW DRAW STRENGTH FROM THE UNITY WE HAVE FORGED...

...LET US WORK TOGETHER... TO BANISH HOMELESSNESS, ILLITERACY, HUNGER AND DISEASE!

HE BECAME THE CHAIRPERSON OF THE SOUTHERN AFRICAN DEVELOPMENT COMMUNITY (SADCC). HE USED HIS POSITION TO CHALLENGE UNDEMOCRATIC MEMBERS.

IT WAS DECIDED TO SEND THE SAS OUTENIQUA TO THE MOUTH OF THE CONGO RIVER. THE SHIP WOULD BE A SAFE HAVEN WHERE MOBUTU AND KABILA COULD NEGOTIATE A TRANSFER OF POWER.

MOBUTU SESE SEKO AND MANDELA WAITED BUT LAURENT KABILA BACKED OUT OF THE MEETING...

...YOU AGREED TO BOARD IN POINTE NOIRE!

I AM CONCERNED FOR MY SAFETY. THE MEETING SHOULD TAKE PLACE IN INTERNATIONAL WATERS...

EVENTUALLY KABILA AGREED TO THE MEETING, BUT PEACE TALKS BETWEEN THE REBEL LEADER AND DICTATOR COLLAPSED.

IN MAY 1997, A DAY BEFORE KABILA'S TROOPS MARCHED INTO KINSHASA, MOBUTU FLED THE COUNTRY...

APARTHEID ERA ATROCITIES WERE STILL HAUNTING THE NATION...

THE TRUTH AND RECONCILIATION COMMISSION (TRC) WAS CREATED IN 1995 TO DEAL WITH THE APARTHEID PAST AND PROMOTE RECONCILIATION.

ARCHBISHOP DESMOND TUTU WAS CHAIR AND ALEX BORAINE HIS DEPUTY.

THE NP WANTED A GENERAL AMNESTY FOR ALL PERPETRATORS. MANDELA REFUSED.

THE TRC WAS DEDICATED IN ST GEORGE'S CATHEDRAL IN CAPE TOWN. NOT EVERYONE WAS PLEASED. SOME WANTED VENGEANCE AND SOME WERE FEARFUL.

OVER THE NEXT EIGHT YEARS A RANGE OF HORRORS WERE DESCRIBED. ORDINARY APARTHEID SECURITY PERSONNEL CLAIMED THEY WERE JUST FOLLOWING ORDERS.

All South Africans face the challenge of coming to terms with the past in ways which will enable us to face the future as a united nation at peace with itself.
To you has been entrusted the particular task of dealing with gross violations of human rights in a manner that ensures that the painful truth is laid bare and that justice is done to the victims within the capacity of our society and within the framework of the constitution and the law.
By doing so and by means of amnesty, your goal is to ensure lasting reconciliation.

I AM TRULY SORRY FOR WHAT I HAVE DONE...

I CAN NEVER HAVE PEACE.

NOT EVERYONE WAS SATISFIED WITH THE OUTCOME. SOME VICTIMS WHO TESTIFIED FELT LET DOWN. THEY DID NOT GET THE REPARATIONS THEY HAD HOPED FOR...

...STRATEGIES NEVER INCLUDED THE AUTHORISATION OF ASSASSINATION, MURDER, TORTURE, RAPE, ASSAULT OR THE LIKE...

PW BOTHA REFUSED TO PARTICIPATE AND DENOUNCED THE TRC AS A CIRCUS.

FW DE KLERK LATER SUCCESSFULLY APPEALED TO COURT TO SUPPRESS THE TRC'S JUDGEMENTS ON HIM.

BY THE TIME THE WORK OF THE TRC WAS COMPLETE, IT HAD BECOME CLEAR THAT THE WOUNDS OF THE PAST WOULD TAKE TIME TO HEAL.

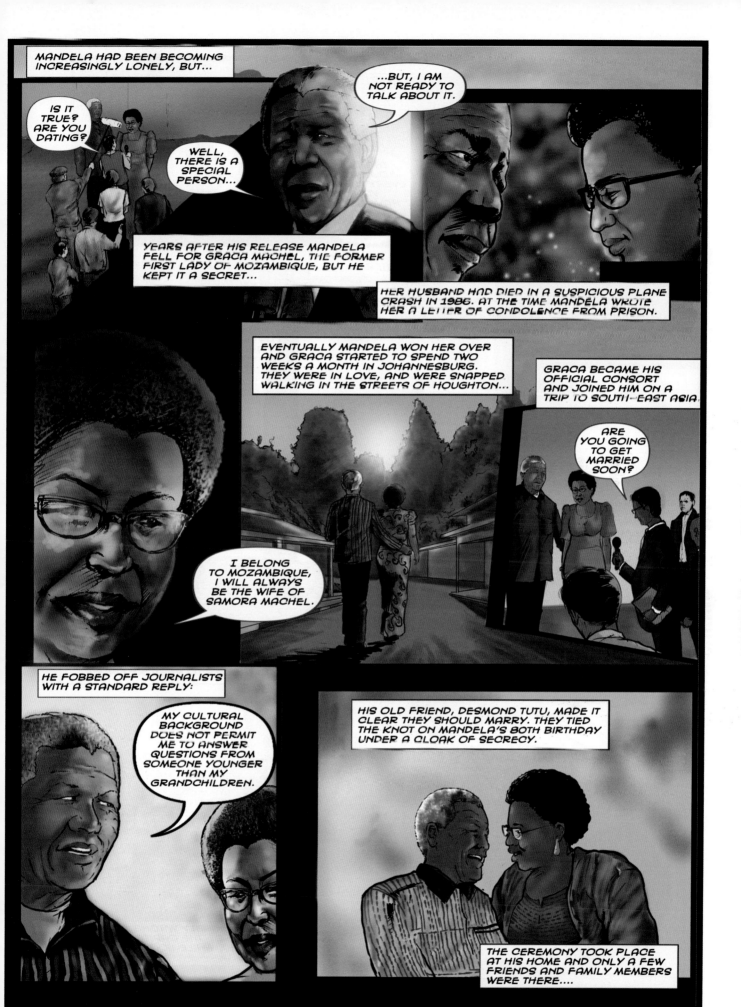

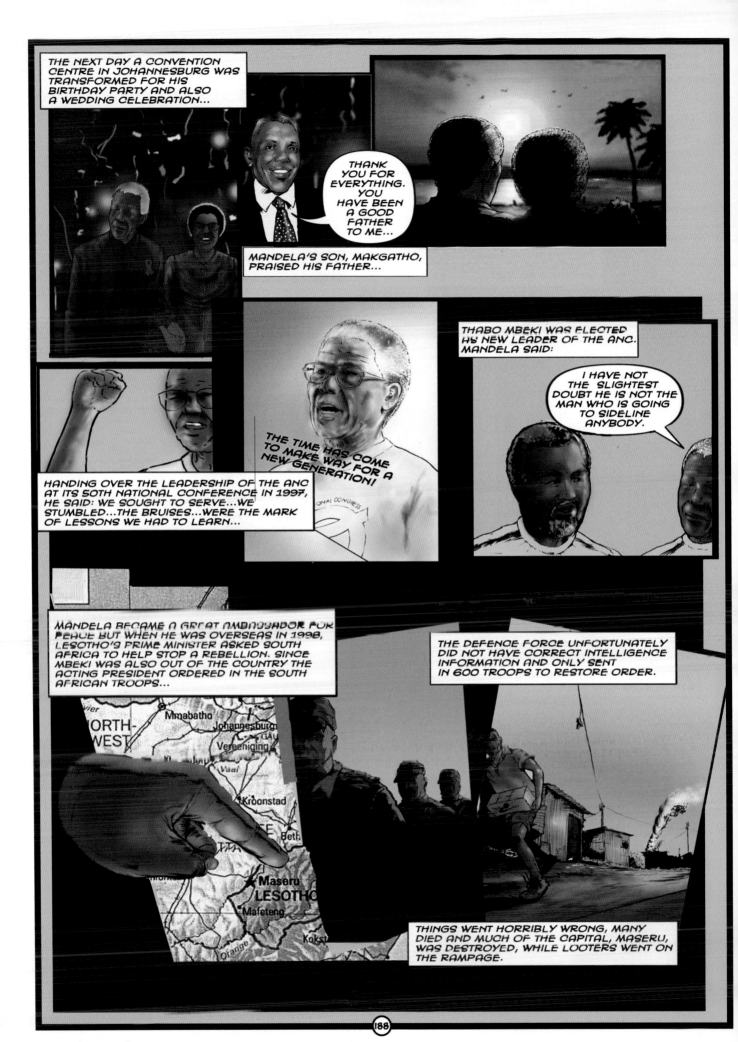

NOTES

Page 3	Frame 2	Mvezo is part of the Thembu kingdom, which forms part of the greater Xhosa nation.

Page 3
Frame 2 Mvezo is part of the Thembu kingdom, which forms part of the greater Xhosa nation.
Frame 3 His umbilical cord was buried right at the front door.
Frame 5 The South African Government controlled traditional chiefs. The government appointed, dismissed and administered, chiefs through local magistrates.

Page 9
Frame 1 Mqhekezweni was also known as "The Great Place".

Page 18
Frame 7 A university education was a rare privilege granted to a few black South Africans.

Page 22
Frame 1 Black South Africans needed official permission to travel across magisterial districts.

Page 26
Frame 4 Wives and children remained in rural areas, sustaining traditional homesteads. Workers earned barely enough to send money back home. This also meant children grew up without their fathers.

Page 28
Frame 4 Pass laws, curfews, high transport costs, separated poverty-stricken communities, high crime and no facilities.

Page 33
Frame 3 As an executive member of the ANC

Page 35
Frame 2 The Government started to enforce segregation with vigour – legislating social interaction and the use of public services, amongst others.
Frame 3 Afrikaner Nationalism was a powerful political and social force. It was determined to destroy what it saw as its greatest enemies – African Nationalism, Communism and white liberalism.

Page 36
Frame 1 Sophiatown in the 1950s was crowded and its residents were mostly poor. It is often described as a vibrant suburb but it became a symbol for the government's resolve to impose total racial segregation.
Last frame To protest against the Act over 10 000 people gathered at the Defend Free Speech Convention in Johannesburg. They resolved to have a one-day strike on 1 May 1950.

Page 39
Frame 5 The proposed stay away failed in parts of the country. For Mandela the struggle had become all-consuming. He was on the executive of the ANC, worked at law firms in the city and eventually qualified as an attorney. Evelyn, on the other hand, was concentrating on family, religion and nursing

Page 42
Frame 6 The laws that put a stop to the campaign included the Public Safety and Criminal Law Amendment Acts.

Page 43
Frame 1 Mandela drafted a document explaining how the ANC could keep in touch with the masses in the event of it being outlawed. It was called the M-Plan.
Frame 5 Removals were carried out under the 1954 Native Resettlement Bill.

Page 47
Frame 2 The women marched to deliver petitions to Prime Minister Strijdom. The police stopped many from even reaching Pretoria.

Page 50
Frame 1 The preparatory examination would determine whether the charges of high treason were sufficient to be heard in the Supreme Court.

Page 52
Frame 1 The defence lawyers were funded by the Treason Trial Defence Fund, which received most of its money from international supporters.

Page 53
Frame 5 Winnie Madikizela was the first African social worker at Baragwanath Hospital in Soweto.

Page 54
Frame 4 At the bride's place, Mbongweni, in Bizana, they were separated as tradition required.

Page 55
Last frame 'Zenani' means "what you have brought to the world".

Page 56
Frame 2 'Africanists' was a term for those who resisted Communism and who favoured a struggle by black Africans.
Frame 6 On 6 April 1959, Robert Sobukwe became the first president of the Pan Africanist Congress. The PAC rejected the Freedom Charter and the policy of working with other race groups.

Page 58
Frame 5 Most of those killed had been shot in the back. In Langa, Cape Town, the protestors were met by a baton charge and two people were killed

Page 60
Frame 1 Thousands of people were detained, including almost every known activist in the country. The Mandela house was raided after midnight.

Page 61
Frame 1 The banned ANC now had to operate along the lines of the M-Plan, relying on secret underground networks of activists.
Last frame 'Kathy' was Ahmed Kathrada's nickname.

Page 62
Frame 4 Zindsizwa means "you are well established".

Using the comic book in the classroom or home

This section is for learners between Grade 4 and Grade 12. The activities focus on different parts of the latest South African school curriculum (CAPS). They are closely linked to the content of the comic book. Nelson Mandela's life story is intricately linked to South Africa's recent history. His actions, words, and values feature in a number of school subjects, notably History, Life Orientation, and the languages.

Nelson Mandela in the school curriculum

Social Sciences

Life Orientation

Languages

The activities that follow are designed to engage young people with this fascinating and essential South African story.

Curriculum links in the Intermediate Phase - Grades 4-6

Social Sciences
The history section of the Social Sciences relates directly to many of the themes covered in the comic book.

Grade 4: Leadership qualities; life story of Nelson Mandela
Grade 5: South African heritage
Grade 6: Democracy and citizenship, the first democratic government in South Africa, national symbols

Life Skills
Nelson Mandela demonstrated many of the values that are part of the Life Skills curriculum.

Grade 4: Respect for others, dealing with conflict
Grade 5: Discrimination, bias, tolerance
Grade 6: Nation building and cultural heritage, gender sensitivity

Languages
Madiba expresses his own 'joy of reading' on the back cover of this book. His facility with language was an essential element of his charisma and achievement.

Grade 4: Reading for enjoyment, listening skills
Grade 5: Visual literacy, knowing the parts of a book
Grade 6: Identifying points of view

Activities for the Intermediate Phase

Activity 1
Look at the contents page of this book. It is the last brown page at the beginning of the book.

1. How many chapters are in the book? _____

2. What is an index? Use the word "alphabet" in your answer. _____
_____
_____

3. Find a word on the contents page that is new to you.
a. Look up the meaning of this word in your dictionary.
b. Write down the word and its meaning on the lines to follow. _____
_____

Activity 2
Turn to page 1 of the book.
1. Fill in the missing words on the line below. This is the title of the chapter.
A _____ of the _____ Cape.

2. What is the meaning of this title? _____
_____
_____

3. Who do you think is the boy in the picture? _____
_____

4. Nelson Mandela and the boy both seem to be thinking about something.
   a. Write one thing the boy could be thinking. _____
_____

   b. Write one thing Nelson Mandela could be thinking. _____
_____

Activity 3
1. Look at the map on the next page. Point to the Eastern Cape. The village where Nelson Mandela was born is marked with the letter M. Fill in the other letters to spell the name of the village. _____

2. The present capital of the Eastern Cape begins with the letter B. Write the other letters of this name on the map.

3. Write the full names of the cities with the letters PE and EL.
PE _____
EL _____

A map of modern South Africa

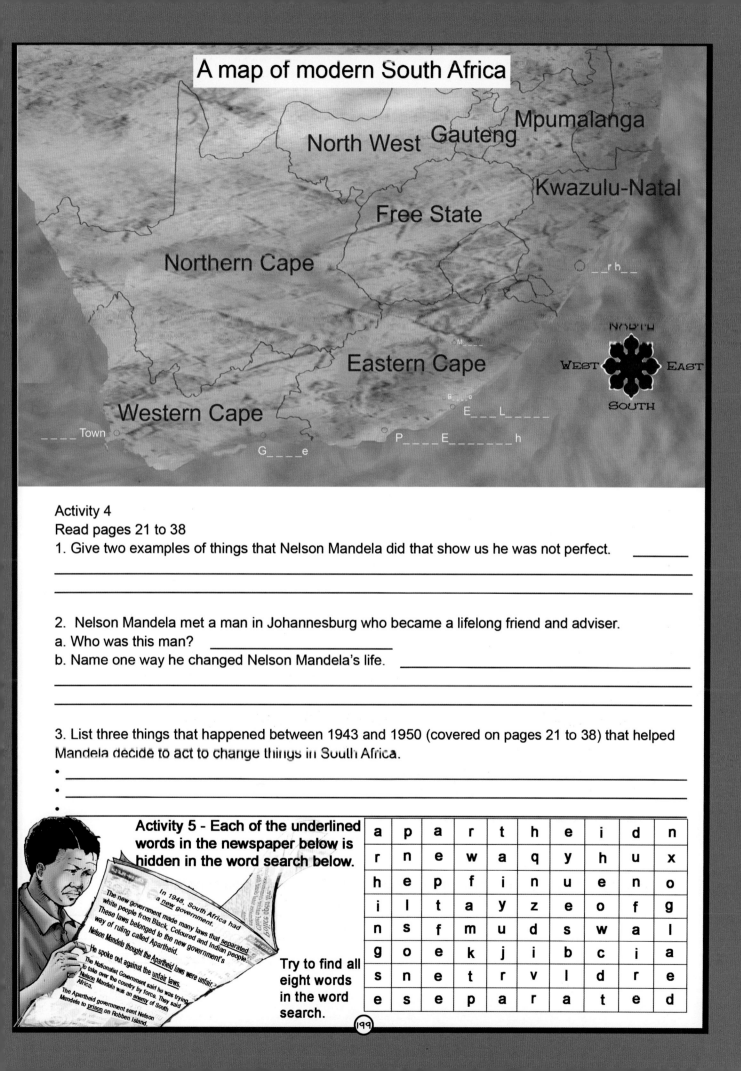

North West   Gauteng   Mpumalanga

Kwazulu-Natal

Free State

Northern Cape

__ r h __ __

Eastern Cape

NORTH

WEST   EAST

SOUTH

Western Cape

E _ _ _ L _ _ _ _ _

____ Town

P _ _ _ _ E _ _ _ _ _ _ _ h

G _ _ _ _ e

Activity 4
Read pages 21 to 38

1. Give two examples of things that Nelson Mandela did that show us he was not perfect. _____

_____

_____

2. Nelson Mandela met a man in Johannesburg who became a lifelong friend and adviser.
a. Who was this man? _____
b. Name one way he changed Nelson Mandela's life. _____

_____

_____

3. List three things that happened between 1943 and 1950 (covered on pages 21 to 38) that helped Mandela decide to act to change things in South Africa.

- _____
- _____
-

Activity 5 - Each of the underlined words in the newspaper below is hidden in the word search below.

In 1948, South Africa had a new government. The new government made many laws that separated white people from Black, Coloured and Indian people. These laws belonged to the new government's way of ruling called Apartheid.

Nelson Mandela thought the Apartheid laws were unfair. He spoke out against the unfair laws.

The Nationalist Government said he was trying to take over the country by force. They said Nelson Mandela was an enemy of South Africa.

The Apartheid government sent Nelson Mandela to prison on Robben Island.

Try to find all eight words in the word search.

a	p	a	r	t	h	e	i	d	n
r	n	e	w	a	q	y	h	u	x
h	e	p	f	i	n	u	e	n	o
i	l	t	a	y	z	e	o	f	g
n	s	f	m	u	d	s	w	a	l
g	o	e	k	j	i	b	c	i	a
s	n	e	t	r	v	l	d	r	e
e	s	e	p	a	r	a	t	e	d

199

Activity 6

The table below shows the dates of some important events in Nelson Mandela's life.

1. Write these three missing events in the correct place in the table.
a. Became president of South Africa
b. Helped bring the Soccer World Cup to South Africa
c. Released from prison

2. The events in the table are in the wrong order. Write out the table in the correct order. Start with the earliest date and end with the date closest to the present.

Date	Event in Nelson Mandela's life
1918	Was born
2010	
1990	
1925	Went to primary school
1994	

Activity 7

1. Match these two qualities with an event in Nelson Mandela's life.

a. works for the good of others _____

_____

b. has courage _____

_____

2. Give an example of an event that shows Nelson Mandela was brave. _____

_____

_____

3. Name an event that showed Nelson Mandela was dedicated to others. _____

_____

4. Write down two other good qualities you think Nelson Mandela showed in his life. _____

_____

_____

5. How can ordinary people follow the example set by Nelson Mandela? List three things.

_____

_____

_____

Curriculum links in the Senior Phase - Grades 7-9

Social Sciences
The comic book covers large parts of the history section of the Social Sciences curriculum.

Grade 7: Colonisation of the Cape

Grade 8: Formation of the South African Native National Congress 1912

Grade 9: The National Party and apartheid; repression and non-violent resistance, Sharpeville, 1976 uprising, 1990 release of Mandela, events leading up to 1994 election

Life Orientation
Themes from the comic book link directly to topics explored in the Life Orientation Curriculum.

Grade 7: Constitutional rights and responsibilities, dealing with abuse

Grade 8: Nation-building, human rights violations, cultural diversity

Grade 9: Citizens' rights and responsibilities, ethical values

Languages
Visual texts such as comics help young people to develop a reading culture. The 'joy of reading' is a wish Nelson Mandela has for all South Africans.

Grade 7: Developing vocabulary, responding critically to texts

Grade 8: Detecting bias, expressing a point of view

Grade 9: Debating issues, engaging with different texts

Activities for the Senior Phase – Grades 7-9

Activity 1

Look at page 35.

1. Who was the leader of the National Party? _____

2. In what year did the National Party come to power in South Africa? _____

3. The National Party started to put in place its policy of total segregation. What did this mean?

_____

_____

_____

4. How did the ANC Youth League plan to demonstrate against the Nationalist Government's apartheid policies? Look at the extracts on the next page for clues.

DAYS BEFORE IT STARTED MANDELA SPOKE ALONGSIDE ANC NATAL PRESIDENT, CHIEF ALBERT LUTHULI AND DR NAICKER, PRESIDENT OF THE NATAL INDIAN CONGRESS.

WE WELCOME ALL TRUE-HEARTED VOLUNTEERS FROM ALL WALKS OF LIFE, WITHOUT THE CONSIDERATION OF COLOUR, RACE OR CREED...TO DEFY THESE UNJUST LAWS...

"I DO HEREBY PLEDGE TO BIND MYSELF TO SERVE MY COUNTRY AND MY PEOPLE... TO PARTICIPATE FULLY AND WITHOUT RESERVATIONS, TO THE BEST OF MY ABILITY..."

26 JUNE 1952, PORT ELIZABETH RAILWAY STATION. RAYMOND MHLABA LEADS VOLUNTEERS THROUGH A WHITES ONLY ENTRANCE...

Activity 2

1. Name one apartheid law the volunteers are protesting in each picture. _____

_____

_____

2. Why did the volunteers want to go to jail? _____

_____

_____

3. Explain why the volunteers' action is an example of peaceful protest. _____

_____

Activity 3

1. Match the words and meanings in the column below.

Words	Meanings
Defiance	Keeping black and white people apart by enforcing laws and rules
Repression	To treat people in a harsh and cruel way
Oppression	Disobeying rules on purpose
Justice	Laws that make sure people are fairly treated
Segregation	Controlling people by force

2. Choose two of the words. Use each word in a sentence about Nelson Mandela's early political activities.

a. _____

_____

b. _____

_____

Activity 4

1. Examine the timeline below.

2. Put these events in the correct decade on the timeline.

o The Defiance Campaign

o The Sharpeville shootings

o Policy of apartheid

o The Soweto uprising

o The formation of the ANC Youth League

o The armed struggle

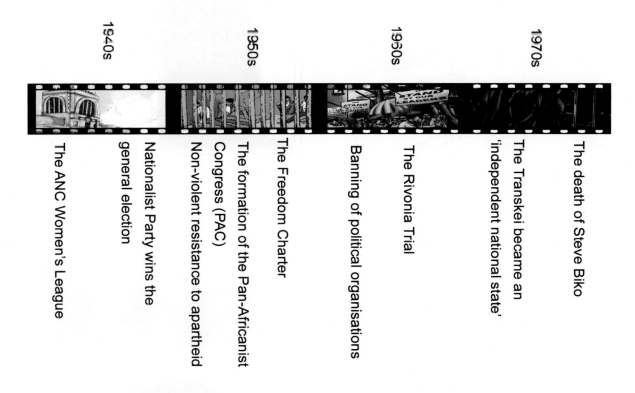

1940s

1950s

1950s

1970s

The ANC Women's League

Nationalist Party wins the general election

Non-violent resistance to apartheid

The formation of the Pan-Africanist Congress (PAC)

The Freedom Charter

Banning of political organisations

The Rivonia Trial

The Transkei became an 'independent national state'

The death of Steve Biko

3. Draw your own timeline to show the 1980s and 1990s.

a. Name three important events in each these decades on your timeline.

Activity 5

1. Where are the below quotes from?

2. Match the quotes with an event on the timeline.

(i) _____

Strijdom, you have touched the women, you have struck a rock, you have dislodged a boulder! You will be crushed!

(ii) _____

FOR THE FIRST TIME SINCE THE UNION... SOUTH AFRICA IS OUR OWN!

Pg35

(iii) _____

UMKHONTO WE SIZWE SPEAR OF THE NATION

A TIME COMES IN THE LIFE OF EVERY NATION WHEN THERE REMAIN ONLY TWO CHOICES SUBMIT OR FIGHT! THAT TIME HAS NOW COME TO SOUTH AFRICA

Pg71

(iv) _____

WE THE PEOPLE OF SOUTH AFRICA, DECLARE FOR ALL OUR COUNTRY AND THE WORLD TO KNOW THAT SOUTH AFRICA BELONGS TO ALL WHO LIVE IN IT...

Pg45

(v) _____

IT IS TIME FOR A PROGRAMME OF TOTAL ONSLAUGHT AGAINST COMMUNIST POWERS!

Pg 119

3. Choose one of the quotes. Explain what events happened directly before the statement was made.

_____
_____
_____
_____
_____

Activity 6
1. Give one example of resistance in the 1980s.

2. How did the South African Government respond to this resistance?

3. Describe two examples of pressure on the South African government to end apartheid that came from outside South Africa.

4. Look at pages 129-30. Nelson Mandela could have been released from prison in 1985 if he had agreed to certain conditions.

   a. What were these conditions?
   b. Why did Nelson Mandela not to agree to the conditions, and decide stay in prison?

Curriculum links in the FET Phase – Grades 10-12

History
The comic book covers large parts of the history curriculum.
Grade 10: Transformations in southern Africa.
Grade 11: Nationalism, ideas about race, apartheid in South Africa 1940s to 1960s
Grade 12: Civil resistance in the 1970s and 1980s, democracy in South Africa, reconciling the past

Life Orientation
Themes from the comic book link directly to topics explored in the Life Orientation Curriculum.
Grade 10: Diversity, discrimination, human rights violations
Grade 11: Democratic participation, democratic structures
Grade 12: Responsible citizenship, responsibilities of levels of government, the role of the media in a democratic society

Activities for the FET Phase

Activity 1
1. The wall on the next page shows some of the apartheid laws and the dates they were passed.
2. Match the statements below with each of the laws.

1. According to this law, people in South Africa were classified according to the South African Government's racial categories – black, white, Indian, coloured.

2. Towns and cities were divided into racial zones. People had to live in areas set aside for their 'racial group'.

3. The government offered inferior education to blacks, Indians and coloured children. One of the main intentions was to make sure that black children remained uneducated, and only qualified to do low-skilled work.

4. This law made it illegal for people from different 'race categories' to marry.

5. Sexual relations between black and white South Africans were forbidden.

The Prohibition of Mixed Marriages Act - 1949

The Immorality Amendment Act - 1950

The Population Registration Act – Act No. 30 of 1950

The Group Areas Act - 1950

The Bantu Education Act - 1953

Activity 2

Look at page 45.

1. The Freedom Charter was written after a meeting of four organisations. Name these organisations.

_____   _____

_____   _____

We, the people of South Africa, declare for all our country and the world to know:
That South Africa belongs to all who live in it, black and white, and that no government can justly claim authority unless it is based on the will of the people.

The people shall govern
All national groups shall have equal rights
All people shall share in the nation's wealth
The land shall be shared by those who work it
All shall be equal before the law
All shall enjoy equal human rights
There shall be work and security for all
The doors of learning and culture shall be opened
There shall be houses, security and comfort
There shall be peace and friendship.

2. Find a line in the Freedom Charter that shows:

a. the people want democracy _____

b. the groups believe in developing education _____

c. apartheid must be abolished _____

3. Choose three demands from the Freedom Charter. List them in the table below. Complete the table using evidence from your own experience of modern South Africa.

Demand from the Freedom Charter	Decide if they are:		Evidence to support your observation
	Met		
	Partly met		
	Not met		

Activity 3

1. The events in the time line below each in some way led up to Nelson Mandela being released from prison.

a. List three examples of civil resistance.

_____   _____   _____

b. List three examples of state repression.

_____   _____   _____

c. List three examples of Nationalist Government political reform.

_____   _____   _____

1976 The Soweto Uprising.

1977 Steve Biko dies in detention; arms embargo imposed on SA by the United Nations Organisation.

1978 P.W. Botha becomes Prime Minister.

1979 Trade Unions are made legal; COSAS is formed.

1980 Thousands of black high school and university students begin a boycott of schools; countrywide protests over wages, rents and bus fares occur.

1981 Ciskei becomes 'independent'.

1982 Right wing breaks away from the National Party to form the Conservative Party.

1983 The National Forum is formed; the United Democratic Front is formed; a whites-only referendum approves the proposed constitution to create a tricameral parliament.

1984 The new constitution comes into effect; the biggest and longest black uprising erupts in the Vaal Triangle; COSAS and FOSATU organise the largest stay-away in South Africa's history.

1985 A State of Emergency is declared in parts of the country; COSAS is banned; many UDF leaders are arrested; white business leaders meet leaders of the ANC in Zambia; COSATU is formed.

1986 COSATU organises a nationwide general strike; a new State of Emergency is declared.

1987 The State of Emergency is extended for another two years; white intellectuals meet the ANC in Senegal for talks; about 200 000 members of the National Union of Mineworkers begin the longest strike in South Africa's history (3 weeks); violence increases between UDF and Inkatha supporters.

1988 The activities of the UDF and other anti-apartheid organisations are banned; the South African army is defeated in Angola.

1989 The State of Emergency is extended for the fourth year; Mandela meets P.W. Botha for talks; Botha has a mild stroke and resigns. F.W. De Klerk becomes president.

Activity 4

Look at page 177.

1. Nelson Mandela publicly supported the Springbok Rugby team in the 1995 Rugby World Cup. Why do you think he did this? _____

_____

_____

2. Consider these points.
- Rugby was a game played and loved by mainly white Afrikaners.
- South Africa had been isolated from international sport because of the sports boycott.
- Reconciliation was an important element in the first ANC government.

_____

INDEX

Published in 2008 by
JONATHAN BALL PUBLISHERS
(A division of Media24 Pty Ltd)
P O Box 33977
Jeppestown
2043

This revised and updated edition published in 2012
Reprinted twice in 2014 and once in 2015

ISBN 978-1-86842-477-1

Design and reproduction by Umlando Wezithombe
Printed and bound by Interpak Books, Pietermaritzburg

NELSON MANDELA
CENTRE OF MEMORY
Living the legacy

The Nelson Mandela Centre of Memory was inaugurated by Nelson Mandela on 21 September 2004. The Centre contributes to the making of a just society by keeping alive the legacy of Nelson Mandela, providing an integrated public information resource on his life and times, and by convening dialogue around critical social issues.

Umlando Wezithombe produces accessible educational comic books. The visual medium is used to cross cultural boundaries and deliver material that addresses a range of literacy levels. Umlando specialises in using the visual medium to address awareness on subjects that include history, HIV/AIDS, healthy living, pandemics, and life skills.

Published by
JONATHAN BALL PUBLISHERS
Johannesburg & Cape Town

ACKNOWLEDGEMENTS

This book began as a series of eight comics distributed free by the Nelson Mandela Foundation in partnership with comic publisher Umlando Wezithombe between 2005 and 2007. The series was a project of the Foundation's Centre of Memory and Dialogue, and was aimed at reaching young South Africans with the story of the life and times of Nelson Mandela, in accessible form. The series drew on a wide range of published work, but also made use of previously unused archival material as well as formal and informal interviews with individuals who appear as characters in the story. We are particularly grateful to Ahmed Kathrada, who acted as special advisor to the series and also assisted with the preparation of this book. His contribution has been immeasurable. The series was made possible financially by a number of generous donors and sponsors – Anglo American, BHP Billiton, the Ford Foundation, GTZ, Independent Newspapers, the Nelson Mandela Legacy Trust (UK), E Oppenheimer and Son, Sasol, and Staedtler.

The Centre of Memory and Dialogue team has relied heavily on the research expertise of Sahm Venter for both the series and this book. Others who have contributed are Anthea Josias, Shadrack Katuu, Boniswa Qabaka and Razia Saleh. Luli Callinicos acted as a consultant for the first five comics in the series.

The Umlando Wezithombe team has been marshalled by Nic Buchanan, and has comprised:
Scriptwriting and research: Santa Buchanan and Andrew Smith
Storyboarding: Santa Buchanan and Pitshou Mampa
Illustrating: Pitshou Mampa, Pascal 'Freehand' Nzoni and Sivuyile Matwa
Inking and colouring: Richie Orphan, Pascal Nzoni, Sivuyile Matwa, Jose 'King' Jungo, Pitshou Mampa and Sean Abbood

The Foundation and Umlando have been supported by an exceptional Jonathan Ball Publishers' team – Francine Blum, Jeremy Boraine and Frances Perryer.

Key reference works utilised by our researchers are as follows:
The World that Made Mandela, Beyond the Engeli Mountains, and *Gold and Workers* by Luli Callinicos, *Drum Magazine, Winnie Mandela – A Life* by Anne Marie du Preez Bezdrob, *Walter Sisulu: I Will Go Singing* by George Houser and Herbert Shore, *The Rivonia Story* by Joel Joffe, *Memoirs* by Ahmed Kathrada, *Mandela* by Tom Lodge, *Long Walk to Freedom* by Nelson Mandela, *Higher than Hope* by Fatima Meer, *A Fortunate Life* by Ismail Meer, *Mandela* by Anthony Sampson, *In Our Lifetime* by Elinor Sisulu, *A Step Behind Mandela* by Rory Steyn, and *Portrait of a People* by Eli Weinberg.

Archival holdings of the following institutions were consulted:
Baileys Historical Archives, Brenthurst Library, Historical Papers (University of the Witwatersrand), the National Archives, the Nelson Mandela Centre of Memory and Dialogue, Robben Island Museum and the University of Fort Hare Library.

Inspiration for this project, of course, came primarily from Nelson Mandela himself. This is his story constellated by numerous other stories. In a profound way the constellation is the story of the country, South Africa, for which Tata Nelson Mandela sacrificed so much. More than this, Tata gave his blessing to the project, launched it with a rousing speech, and shared his memories. The book is a gift to him in his ninetieth year.

Verne Harris
Project Manager
Nelson Mandela Foundation

NOTES

NOTES

NOTES

NOTES